Guitar Magic

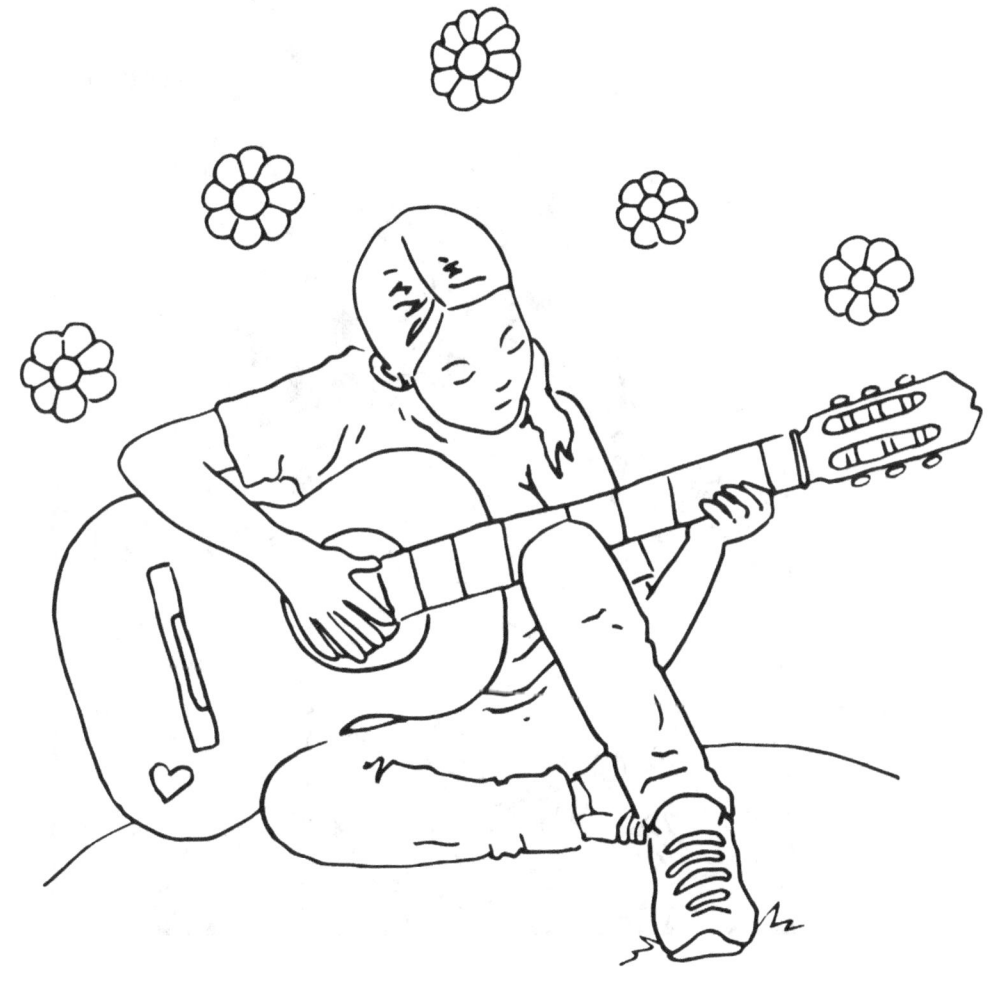

Coloring Book for All
DRAWINGS BY KIMBERLY GARVEY

Cover illustration drawn by Kimberly Garvey and colored by Donna Pecoraro.

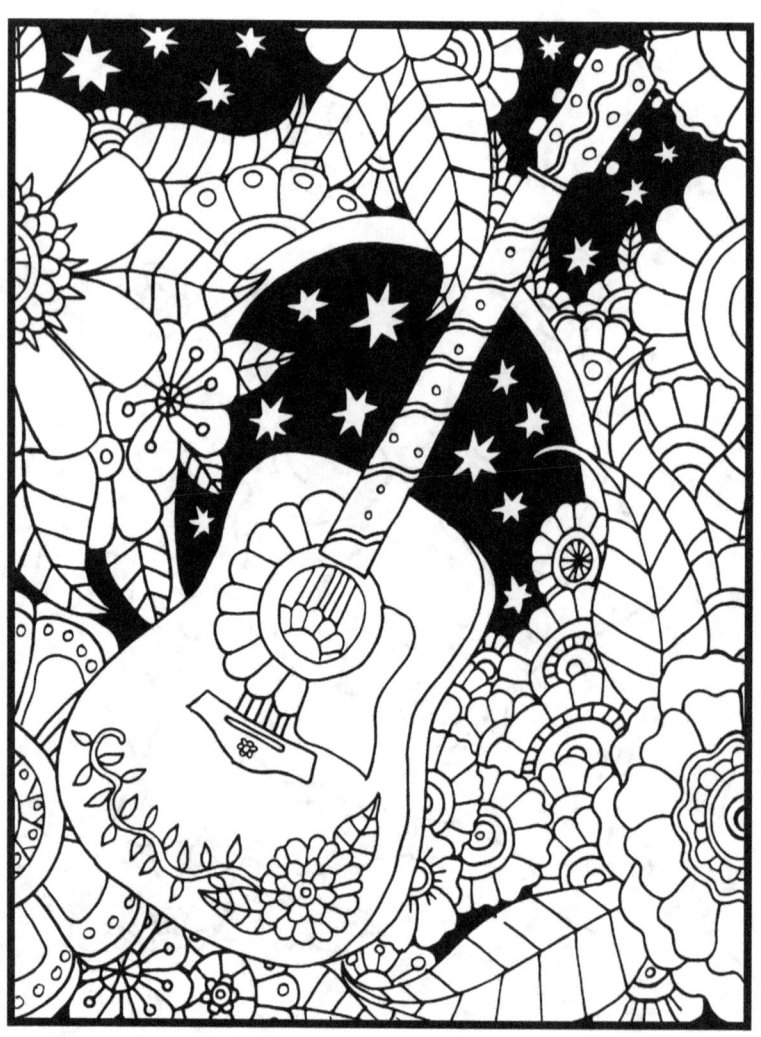

Copyright 2021 by Kimberly Garvey

All Rights Reserved.

No reproduction of any kind without consent.

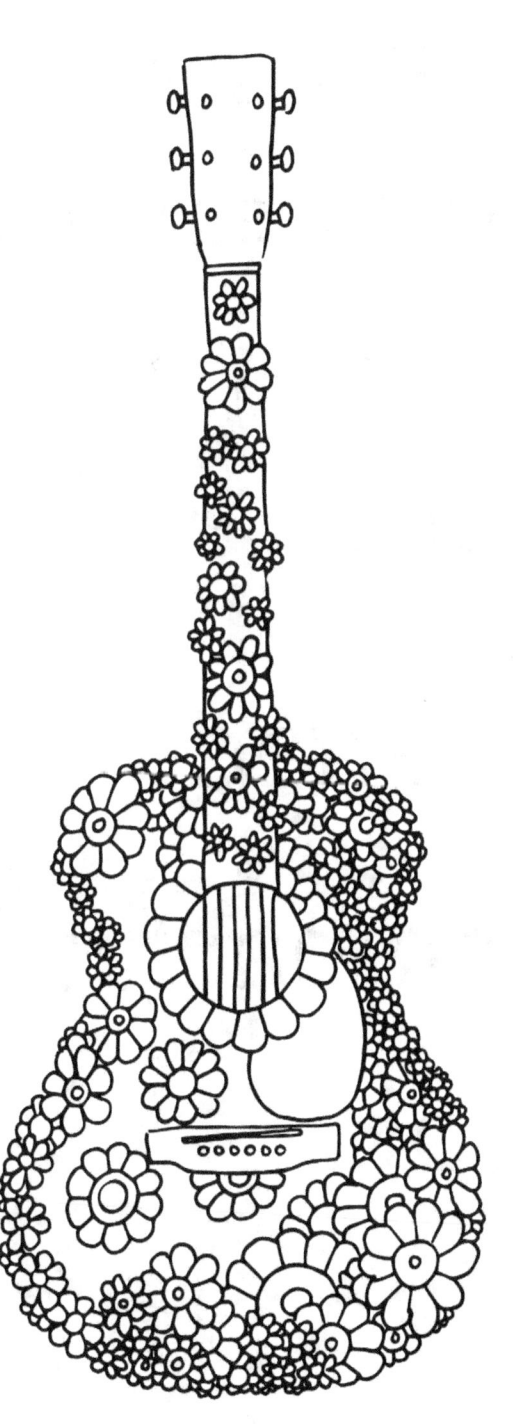

Dedicated to my wonderful husband, Pat Garvey who helped me come up with ideas for this book. ♡

WARNING!!!!

Please put a protection sheet of paper between the pages when using markers to prevent bleed-through.

A protection sheet is included at the back of this book.

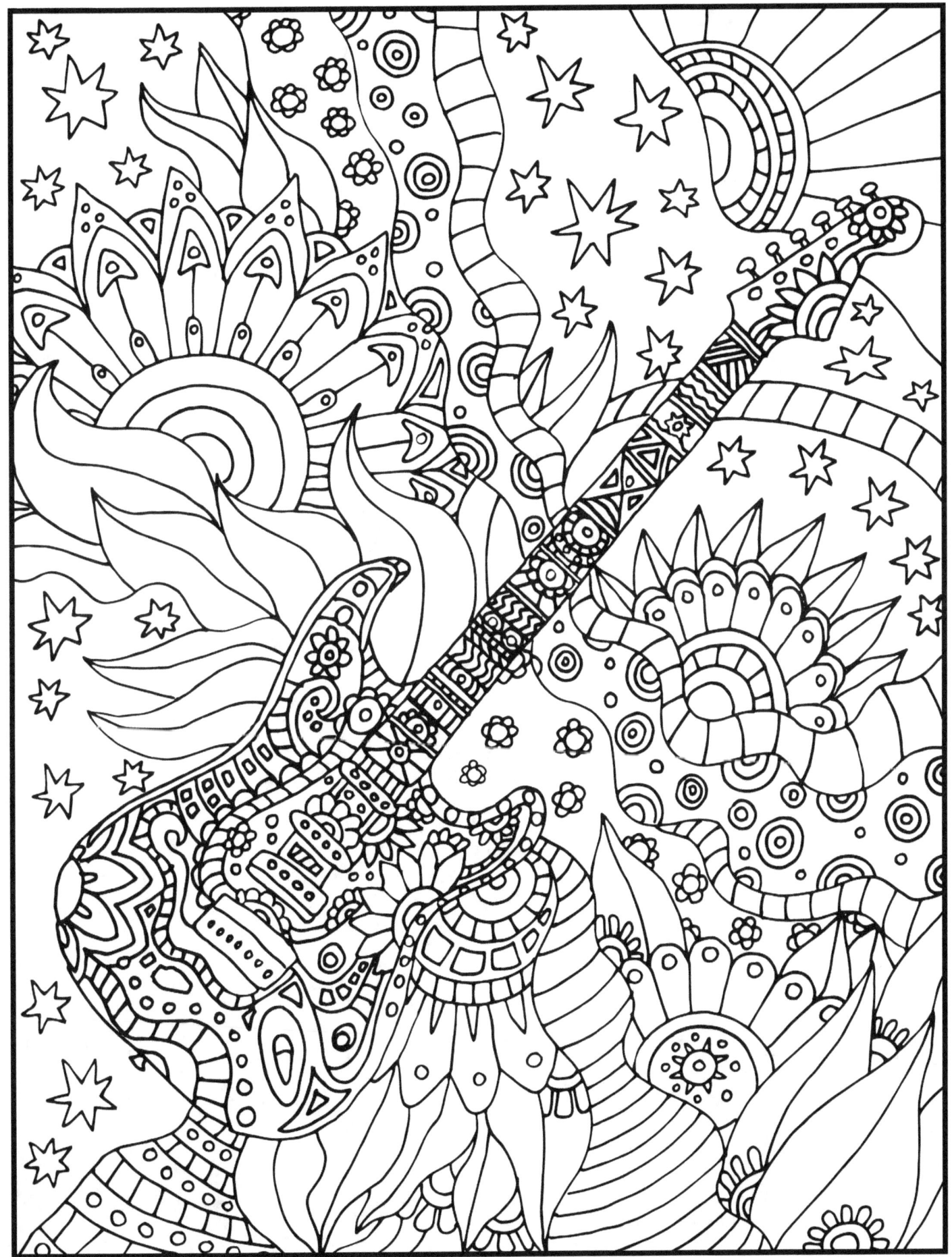

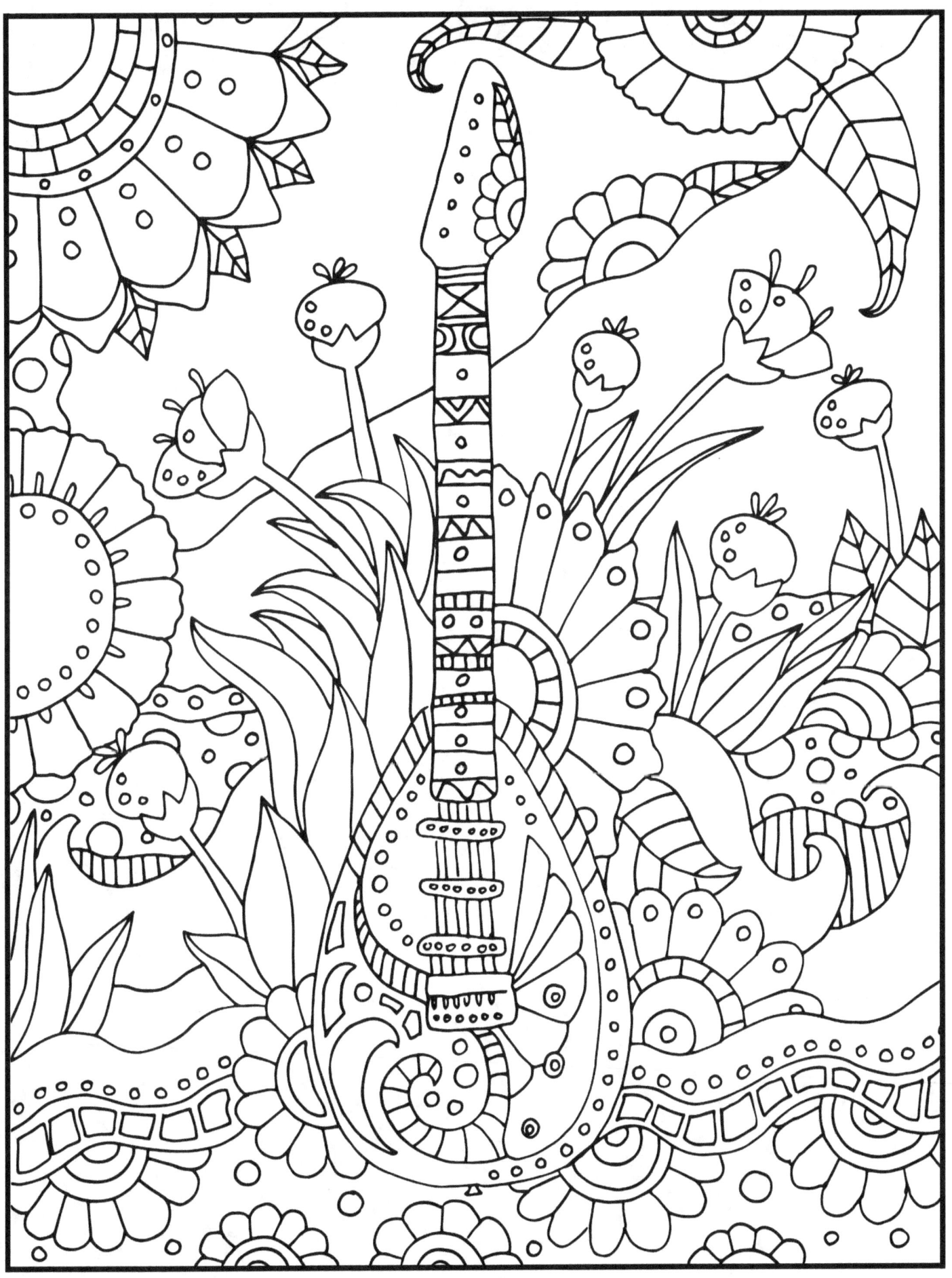

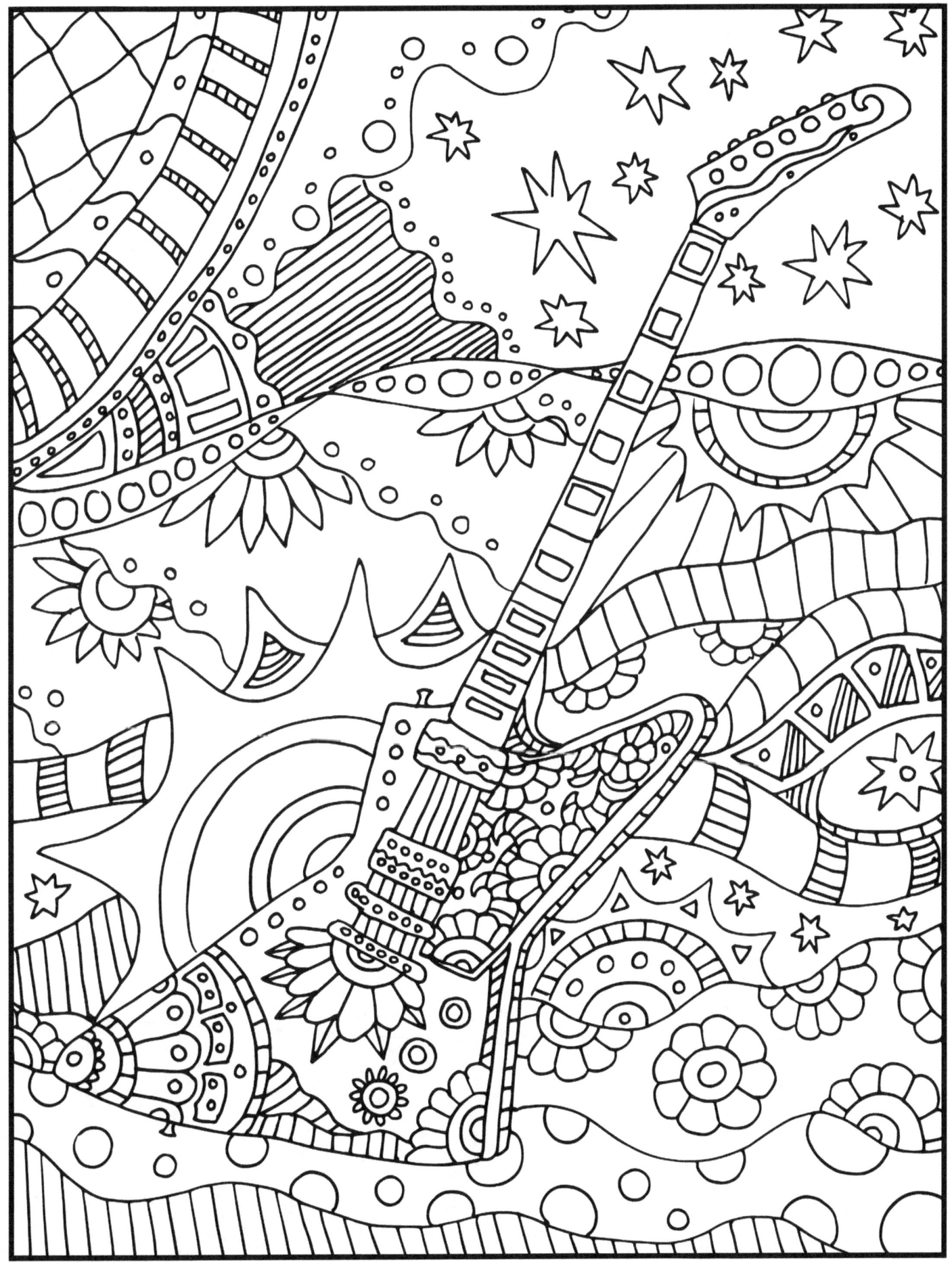

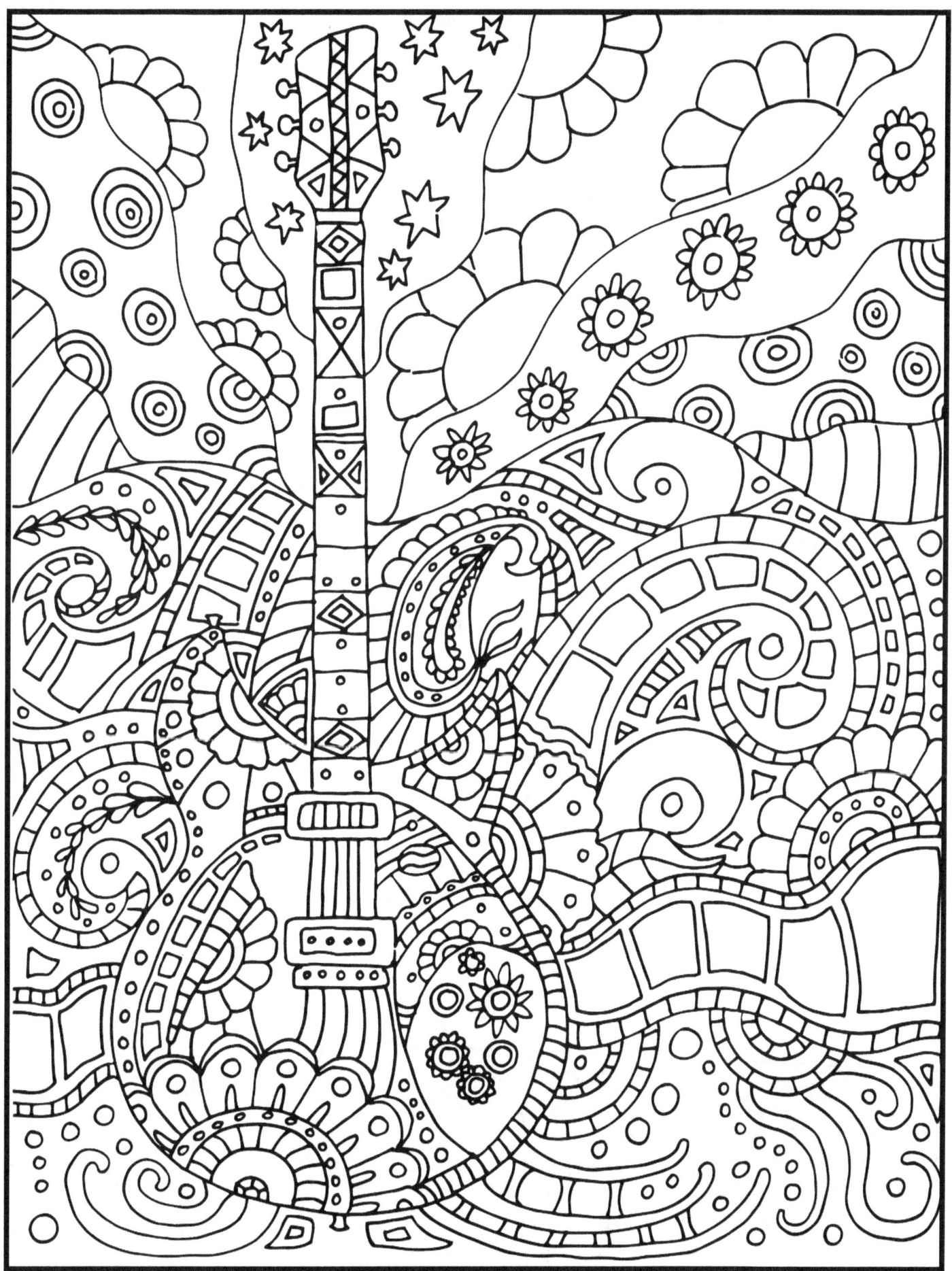

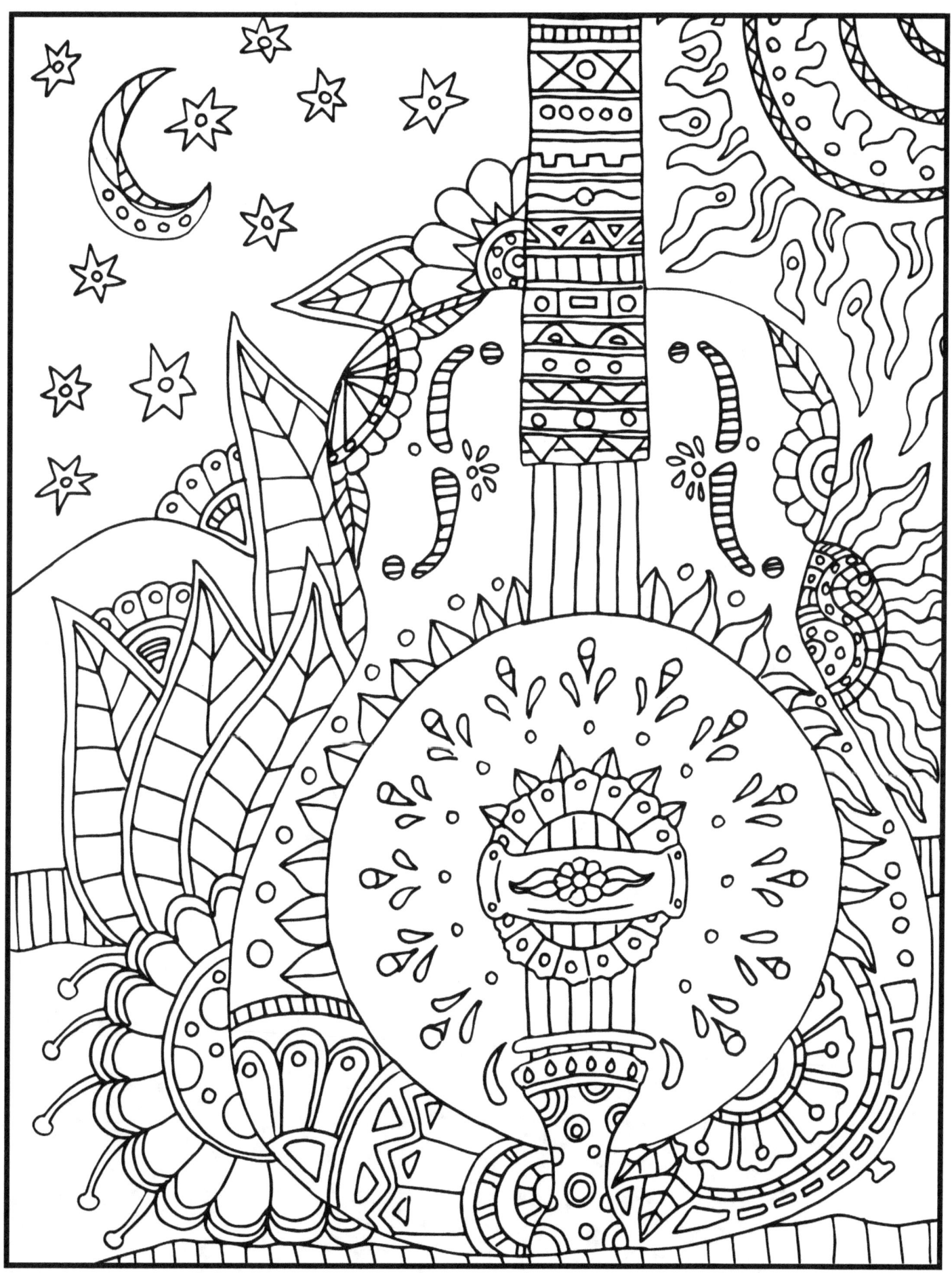

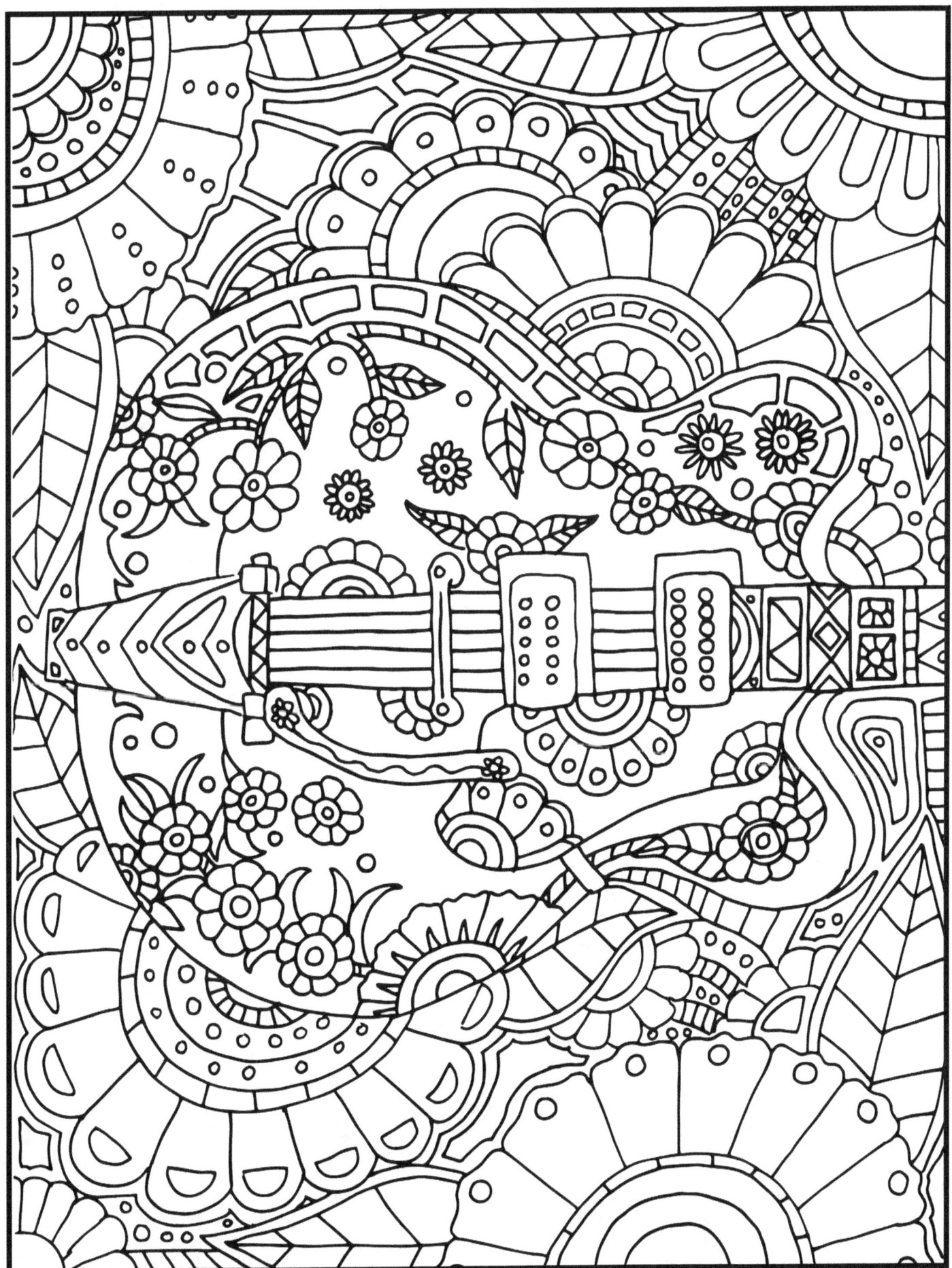

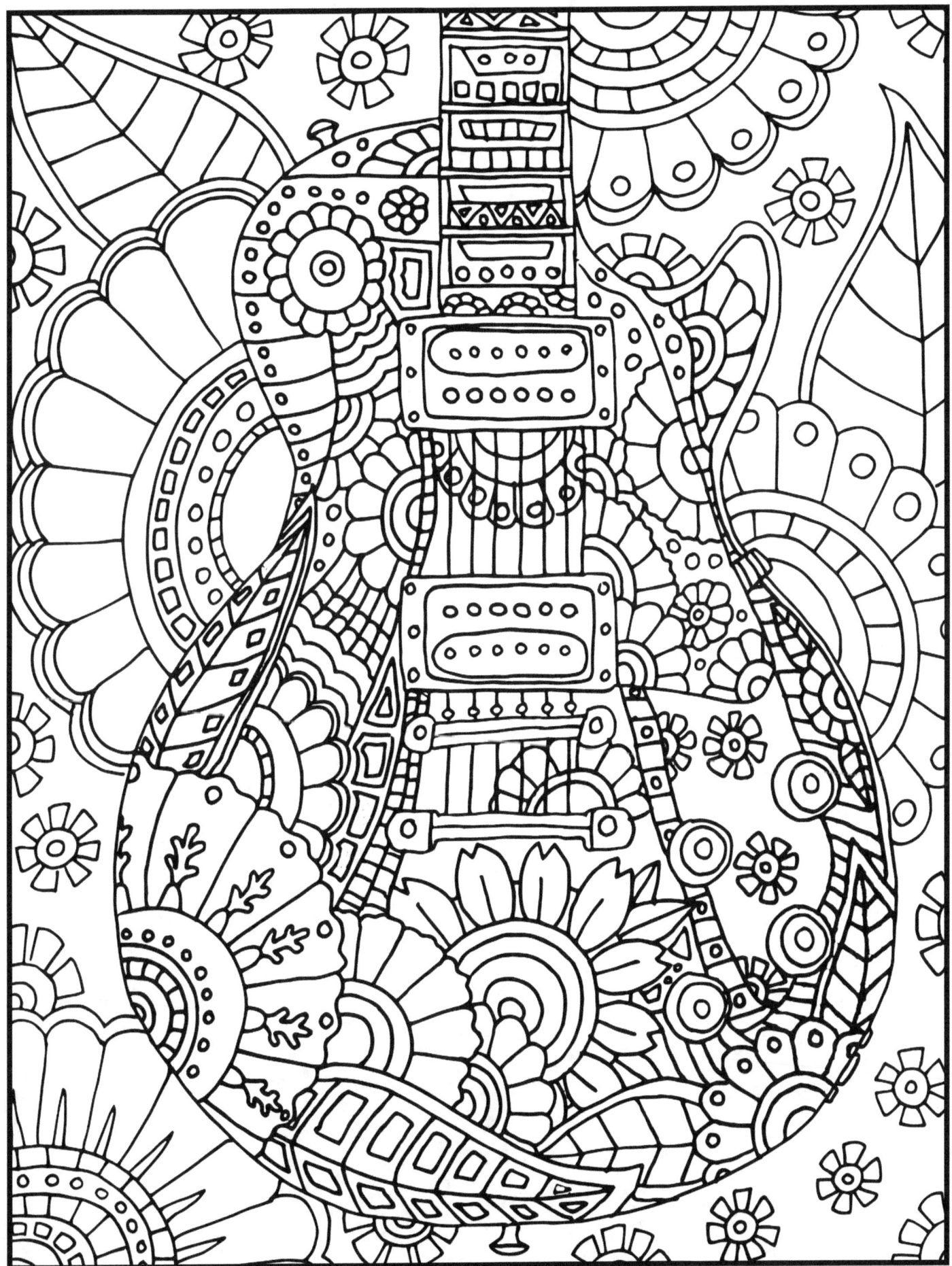

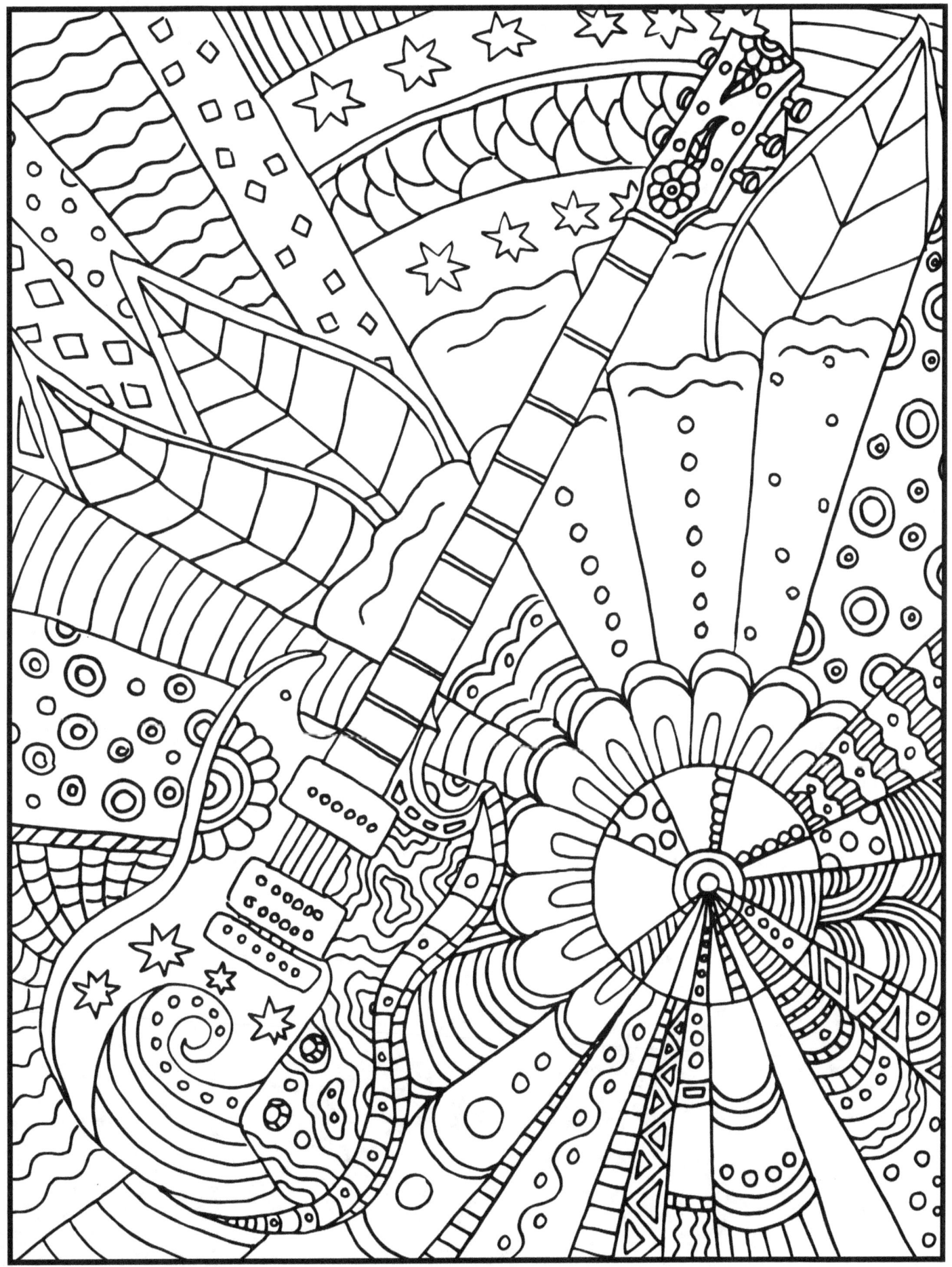

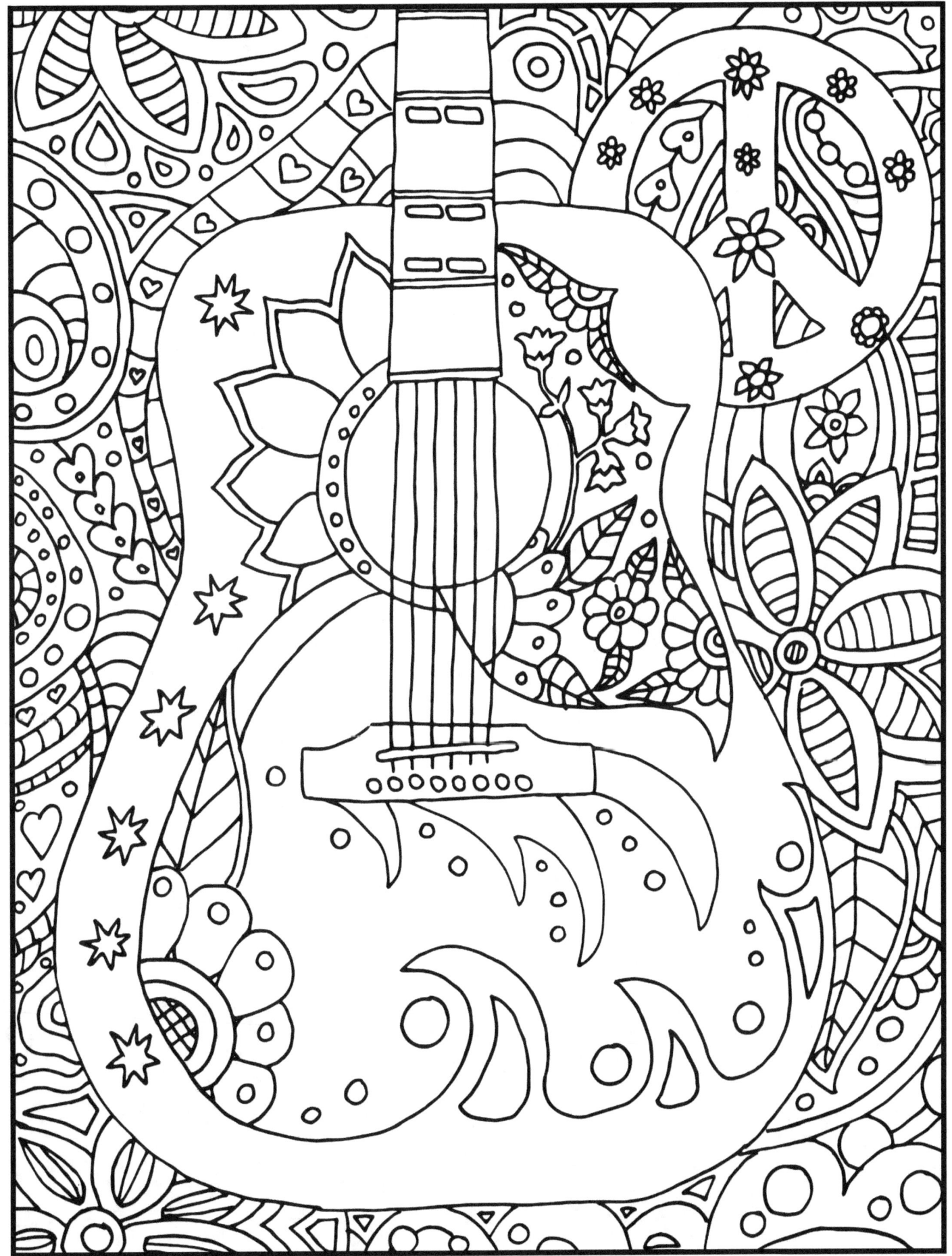

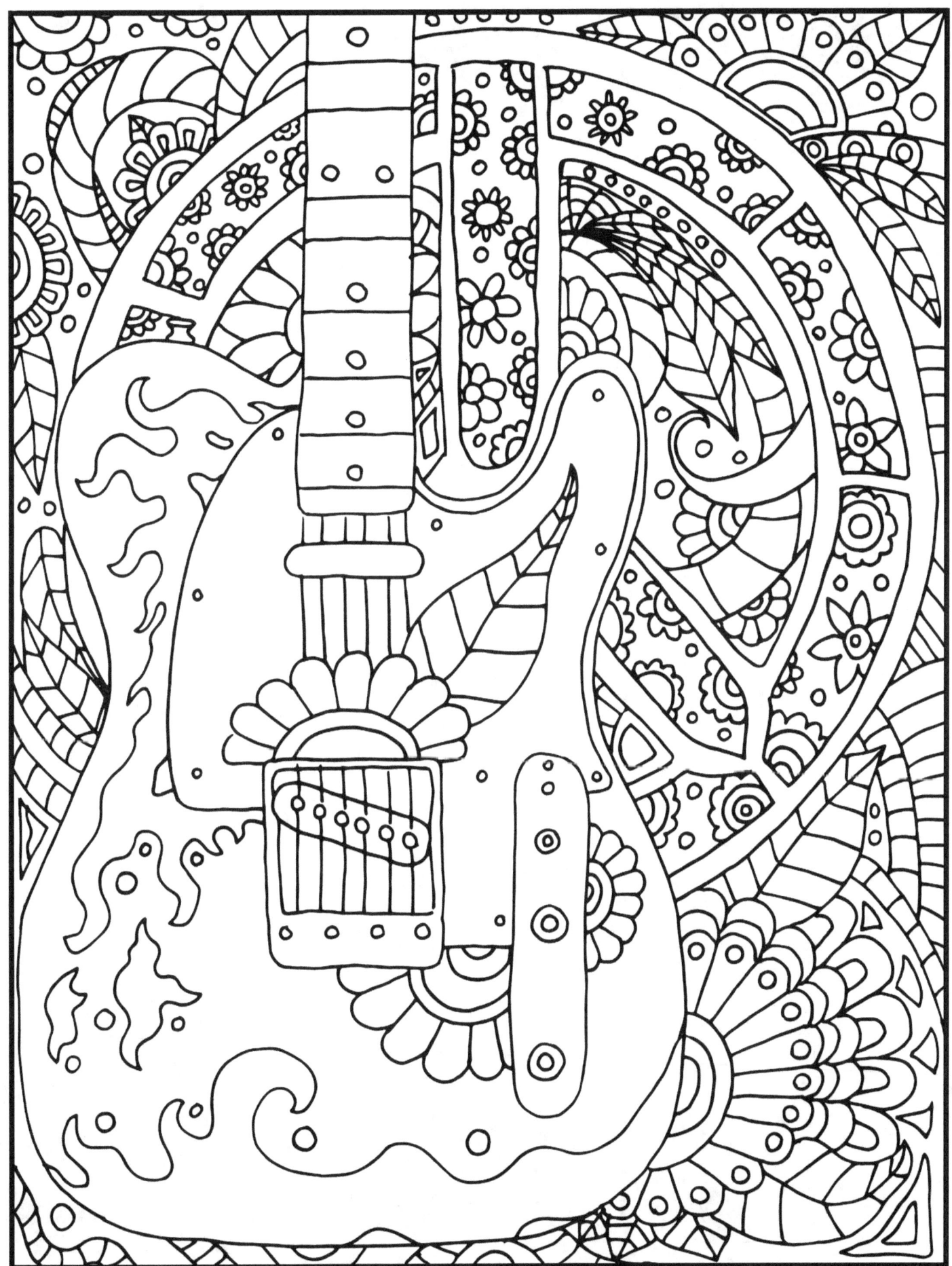

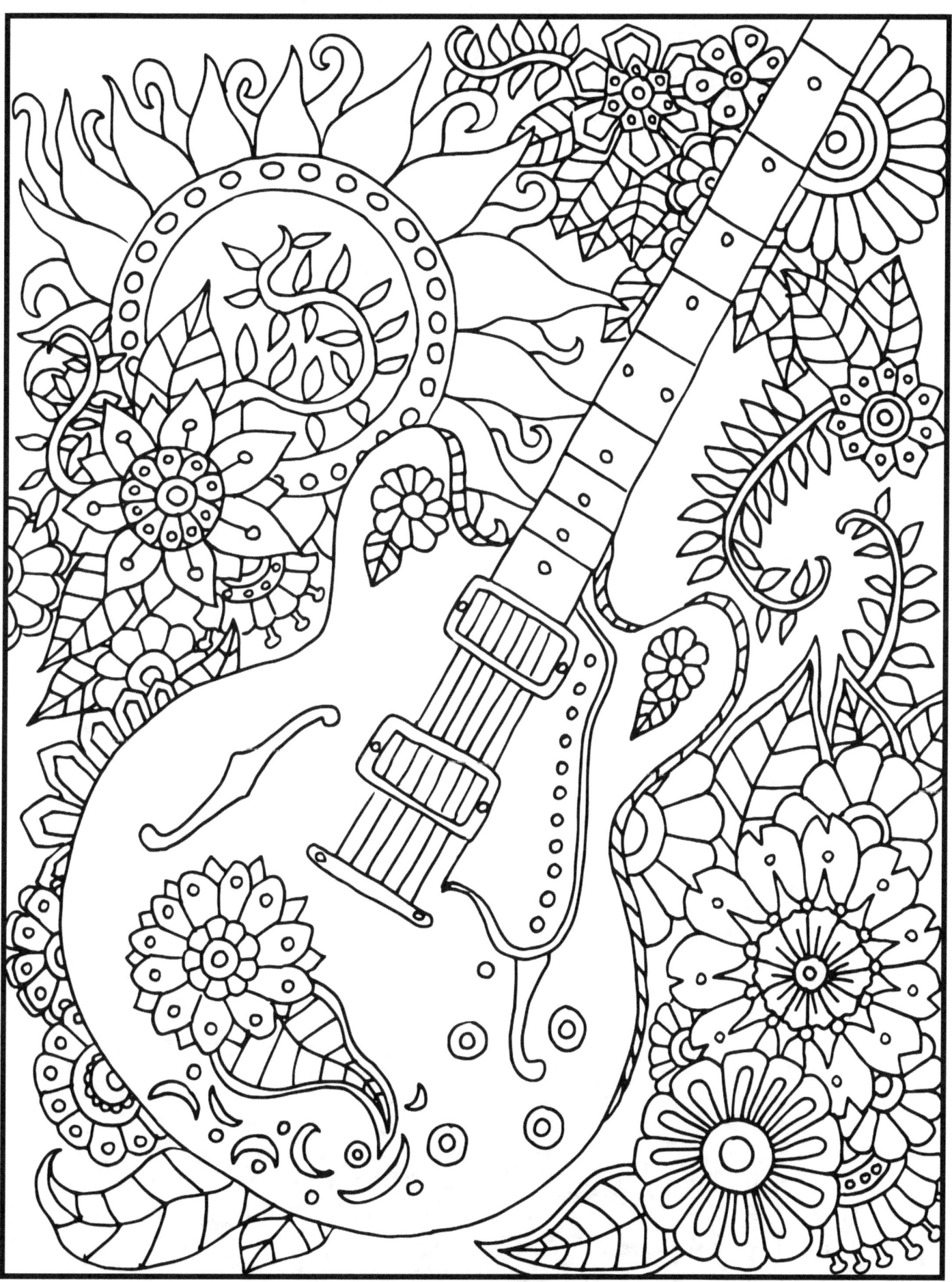

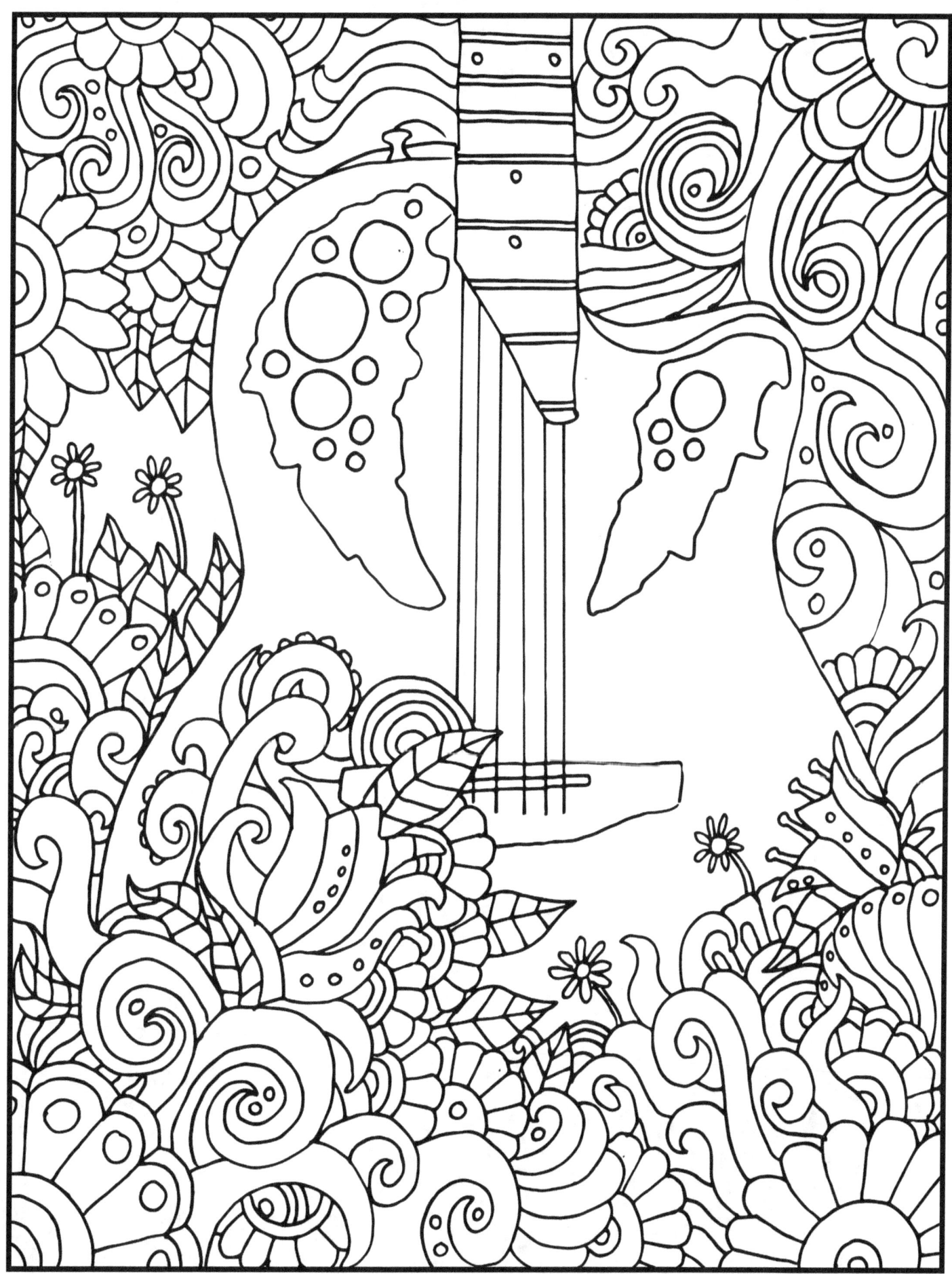

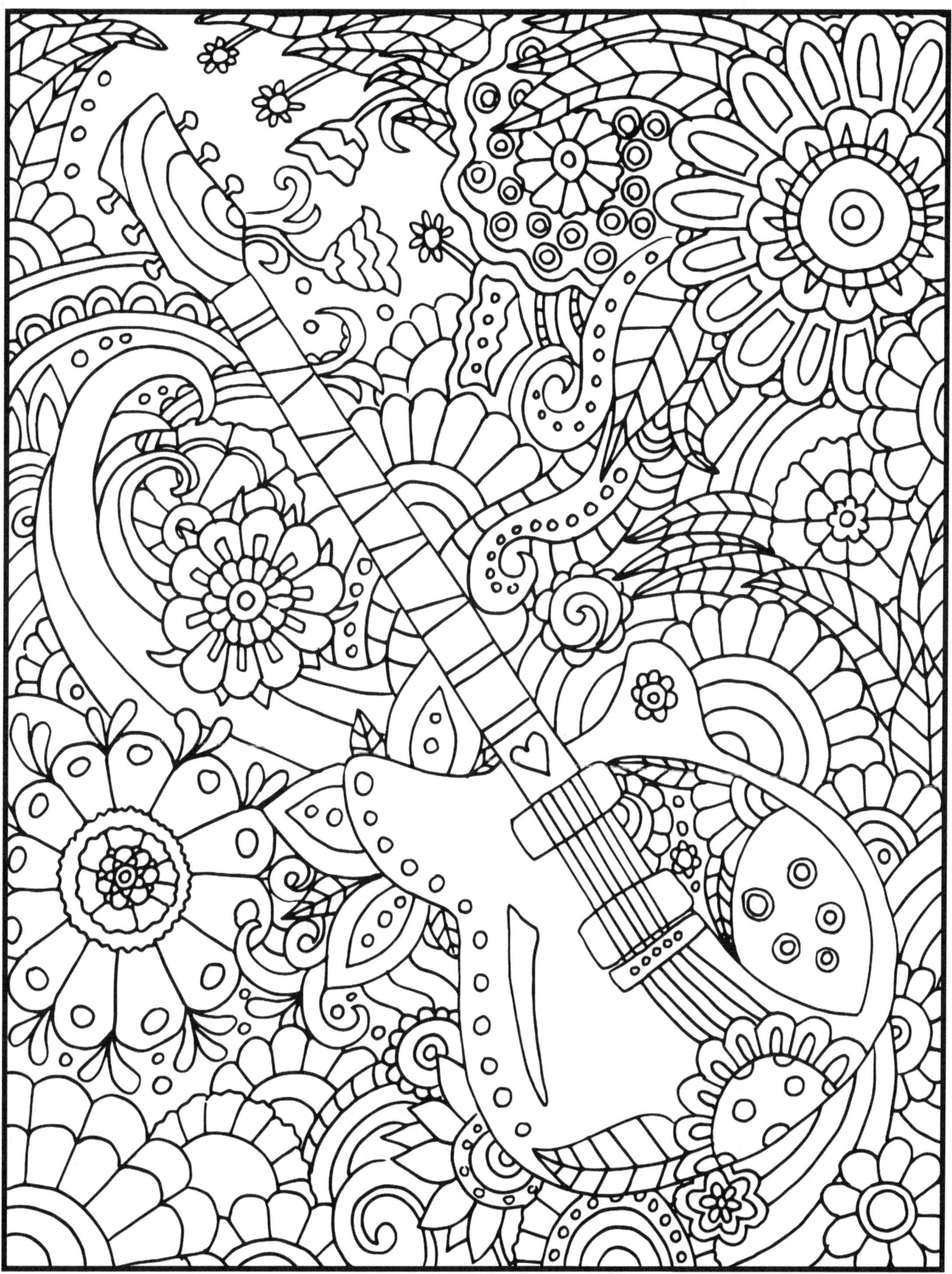

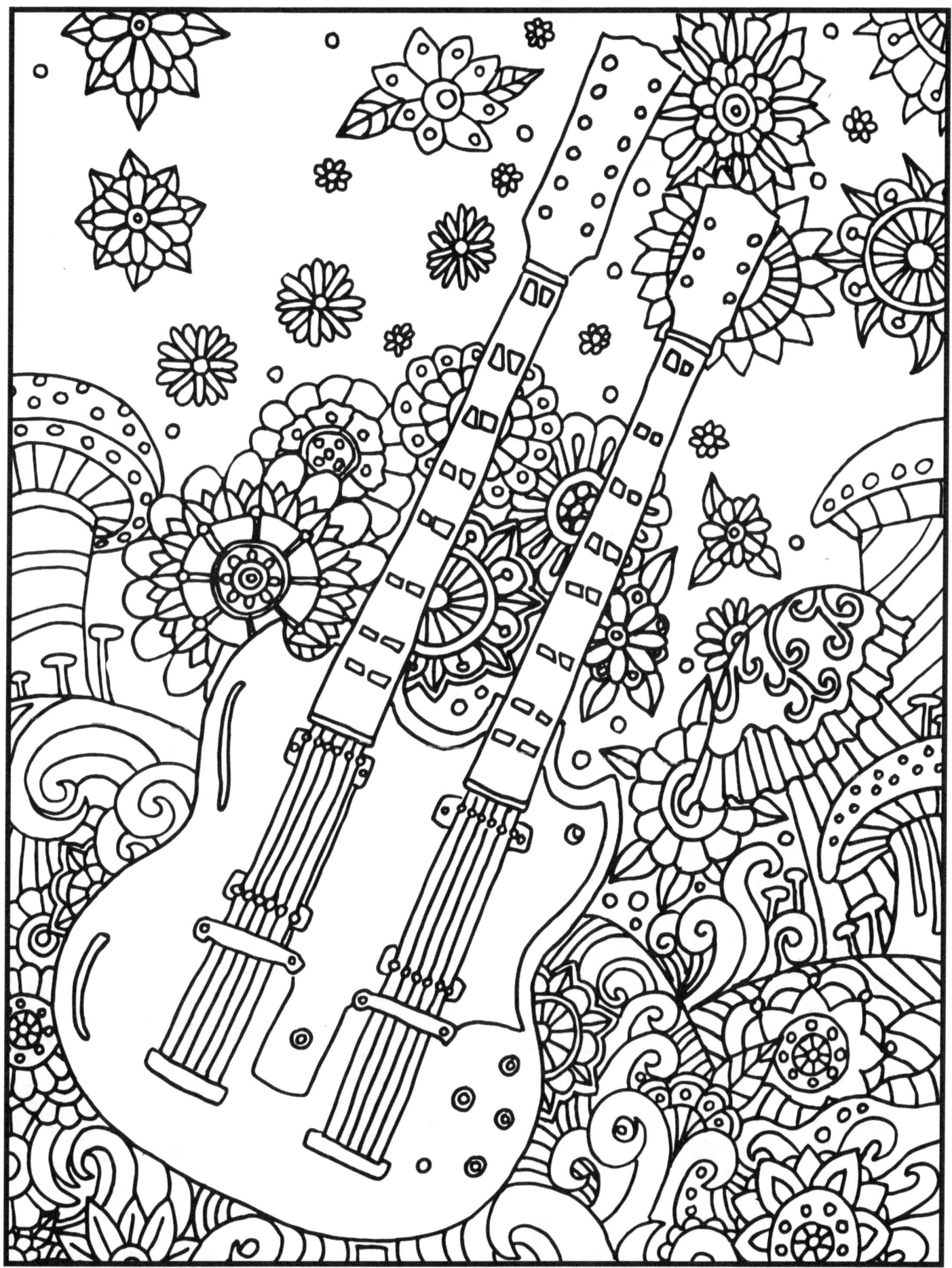

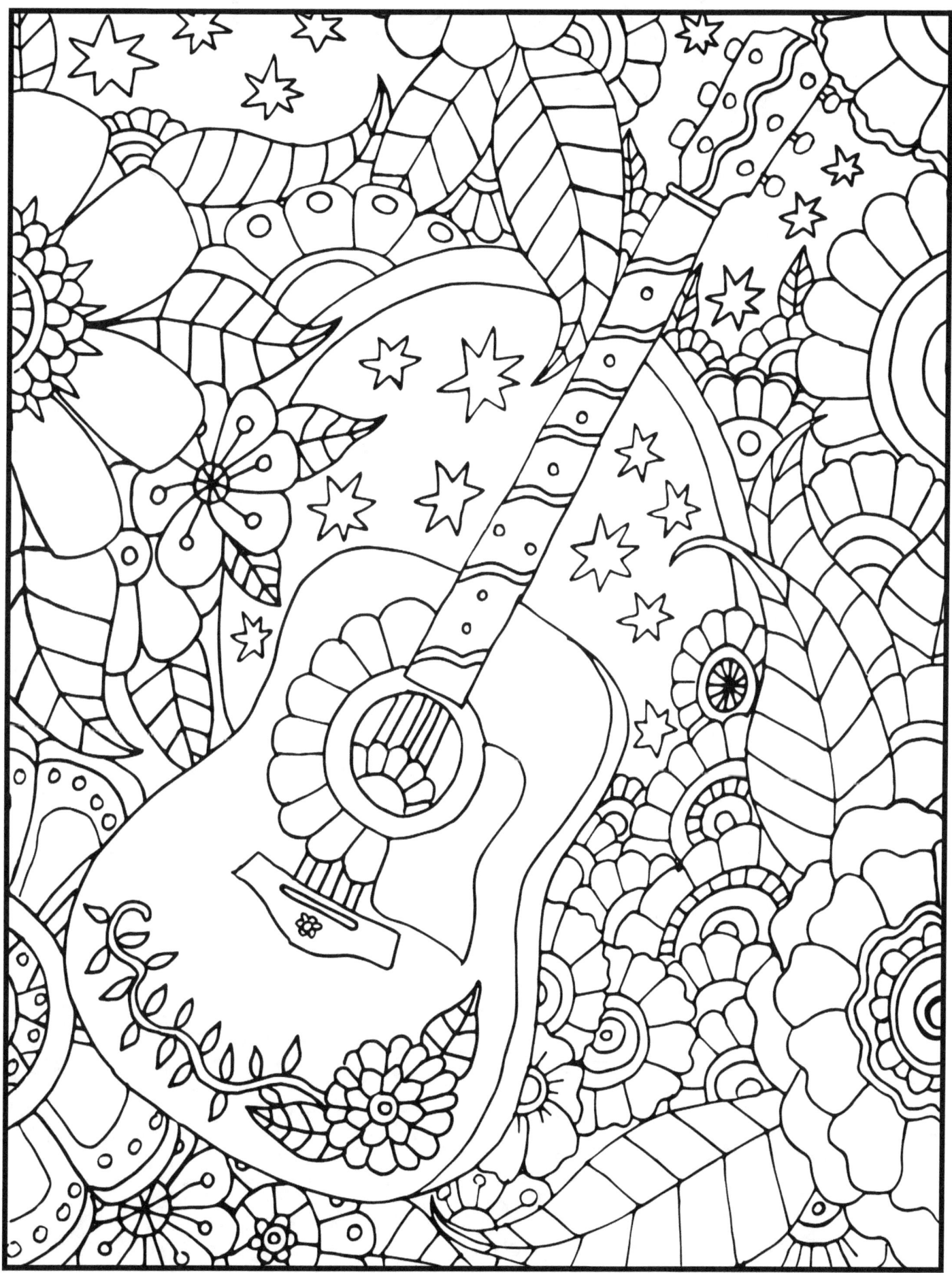

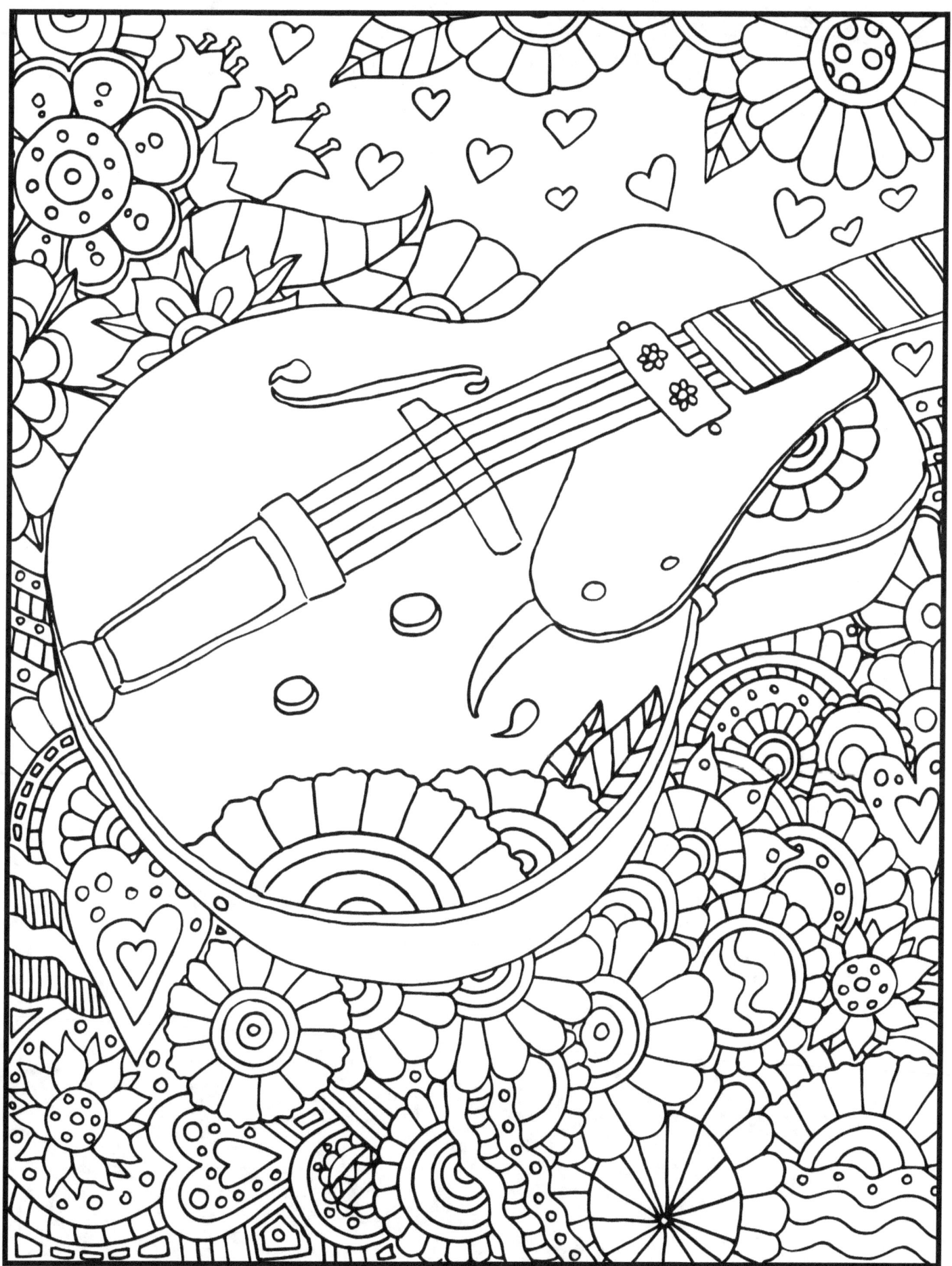

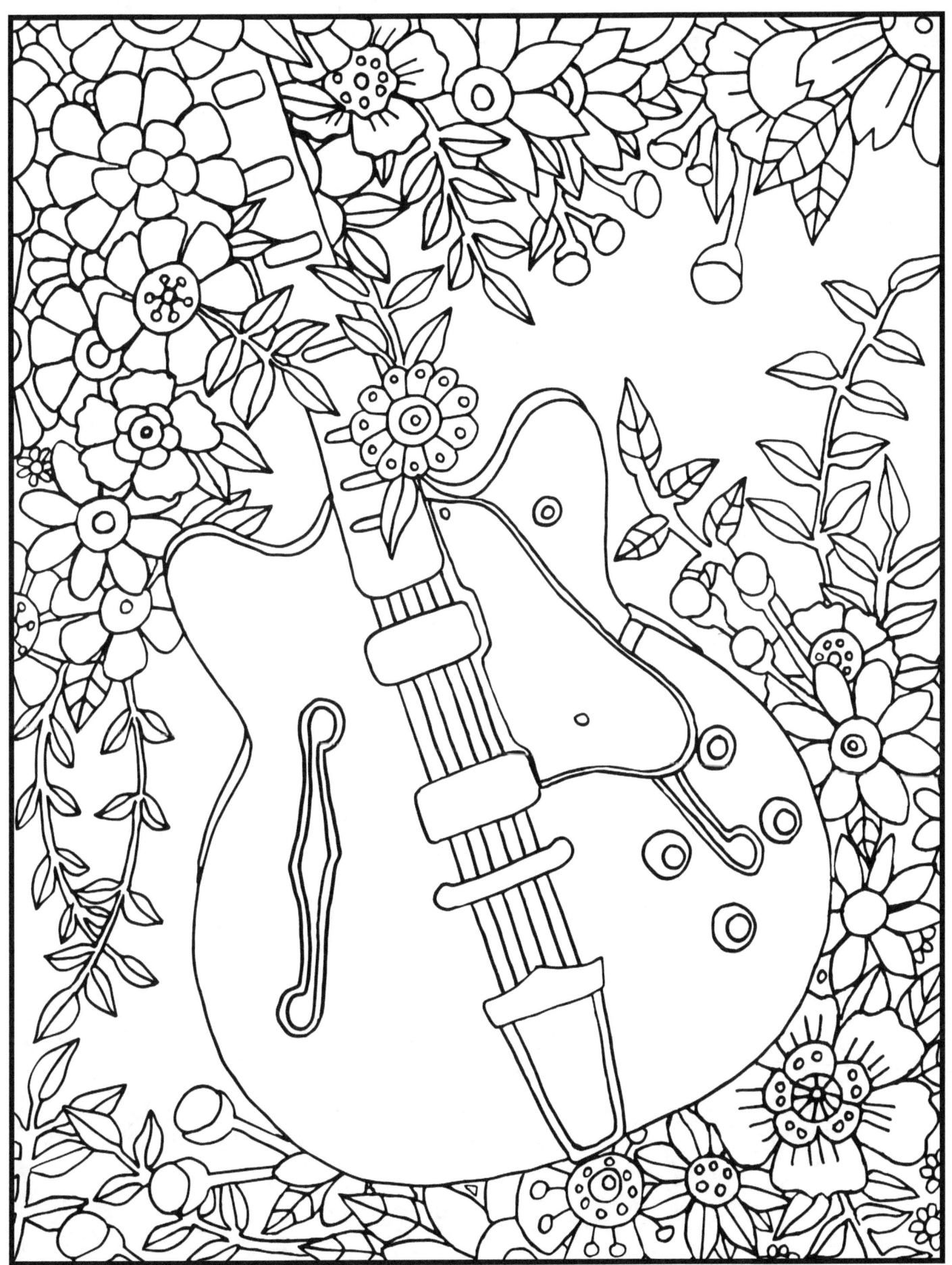

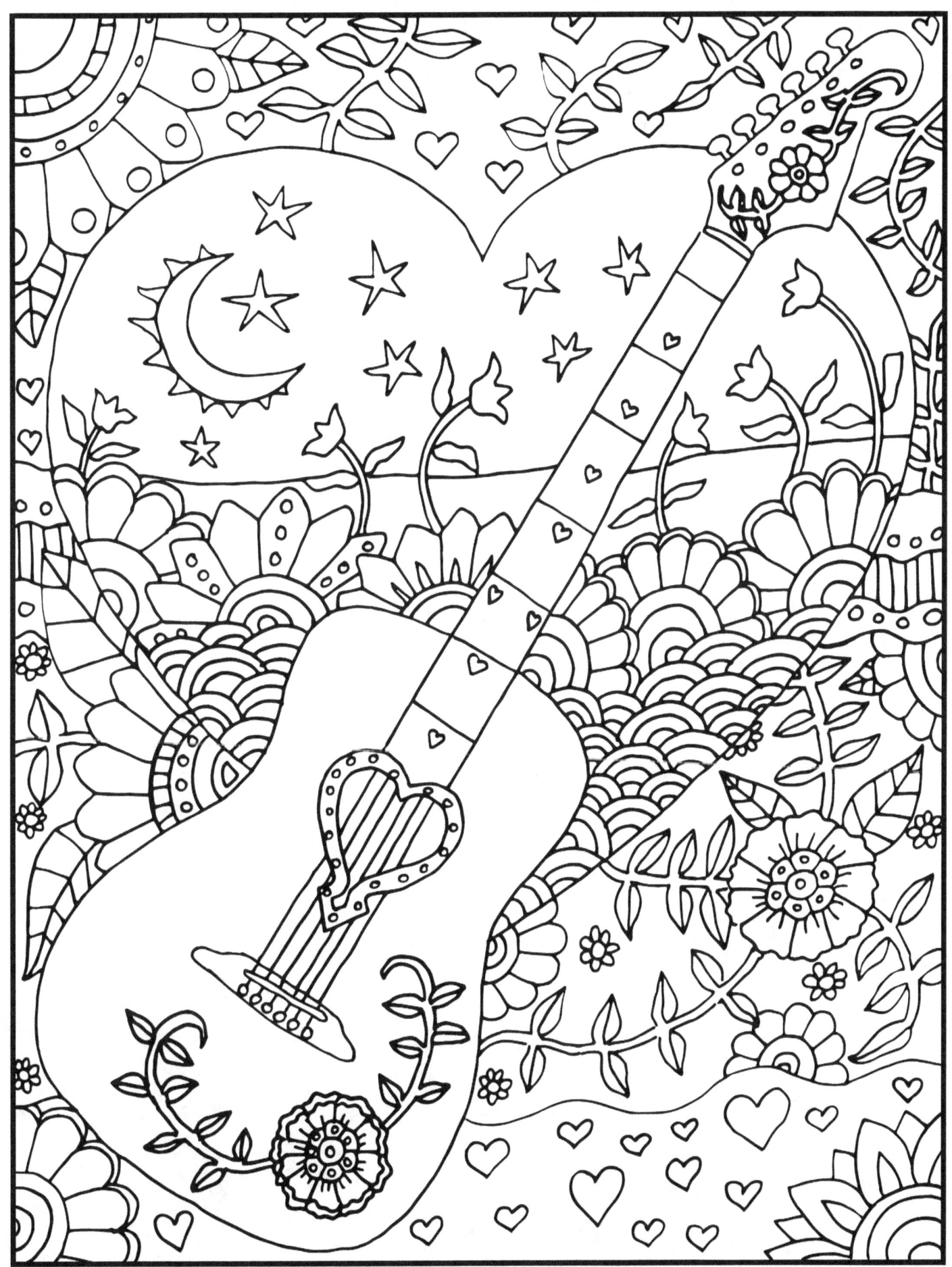

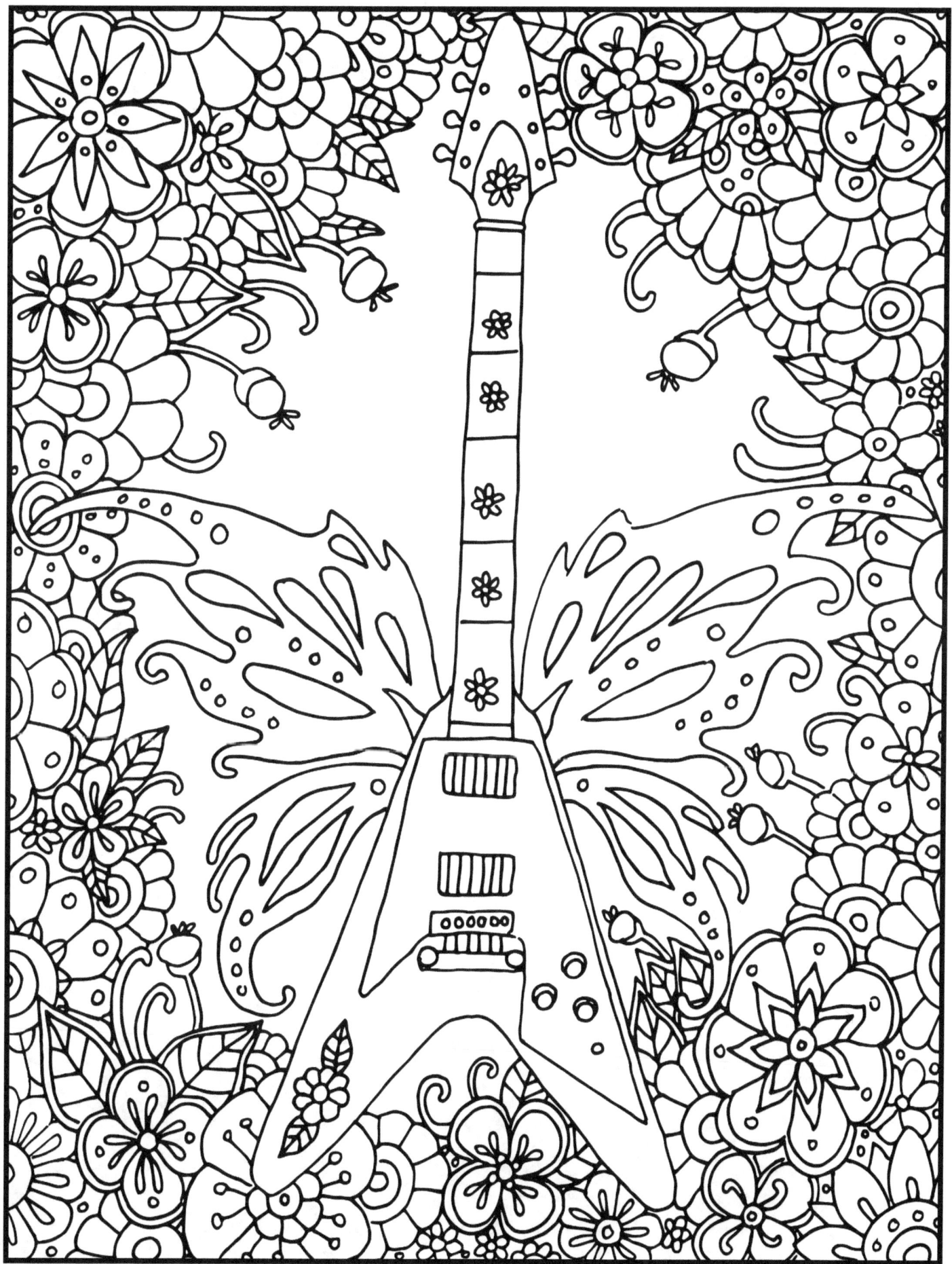

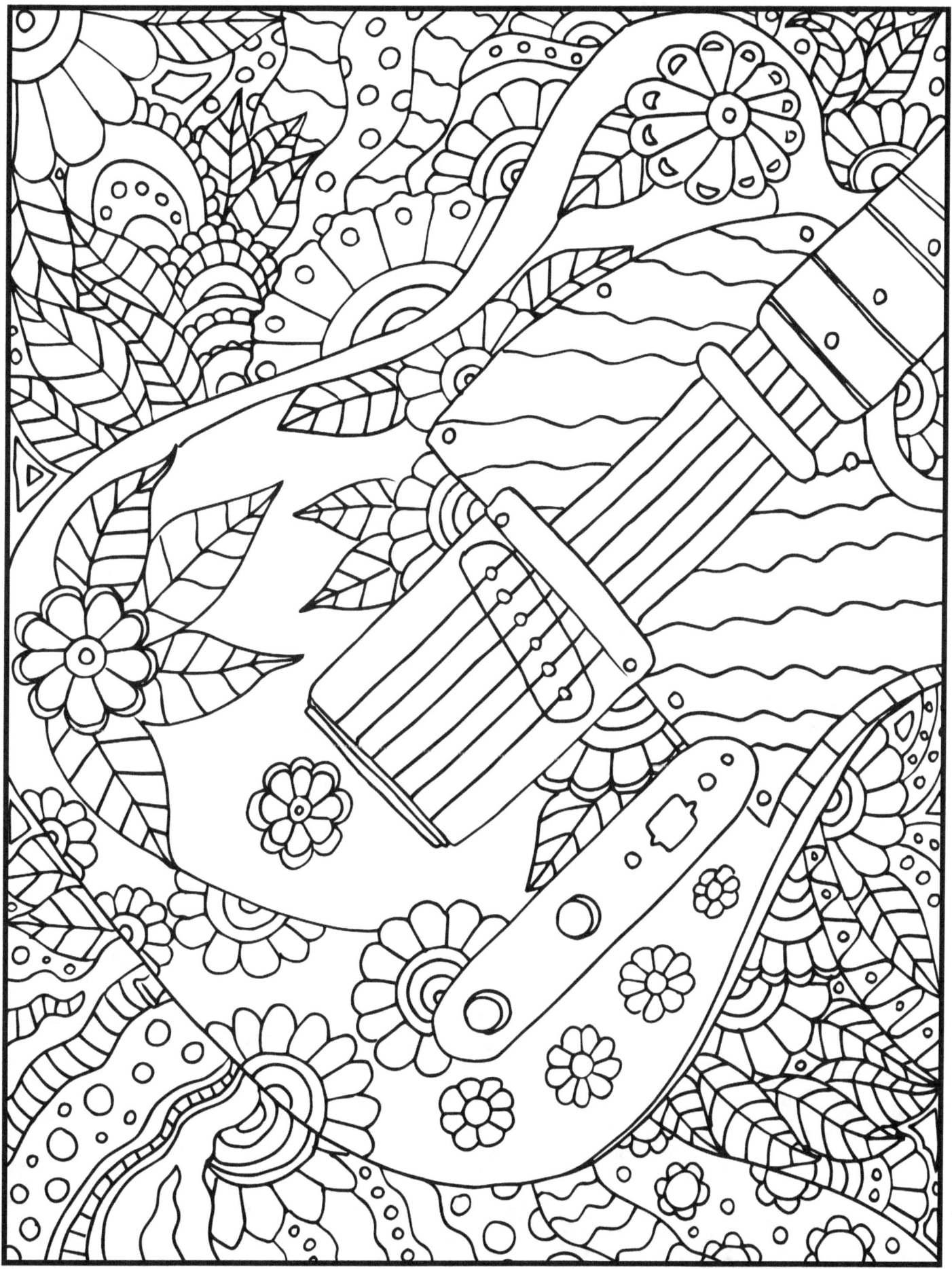

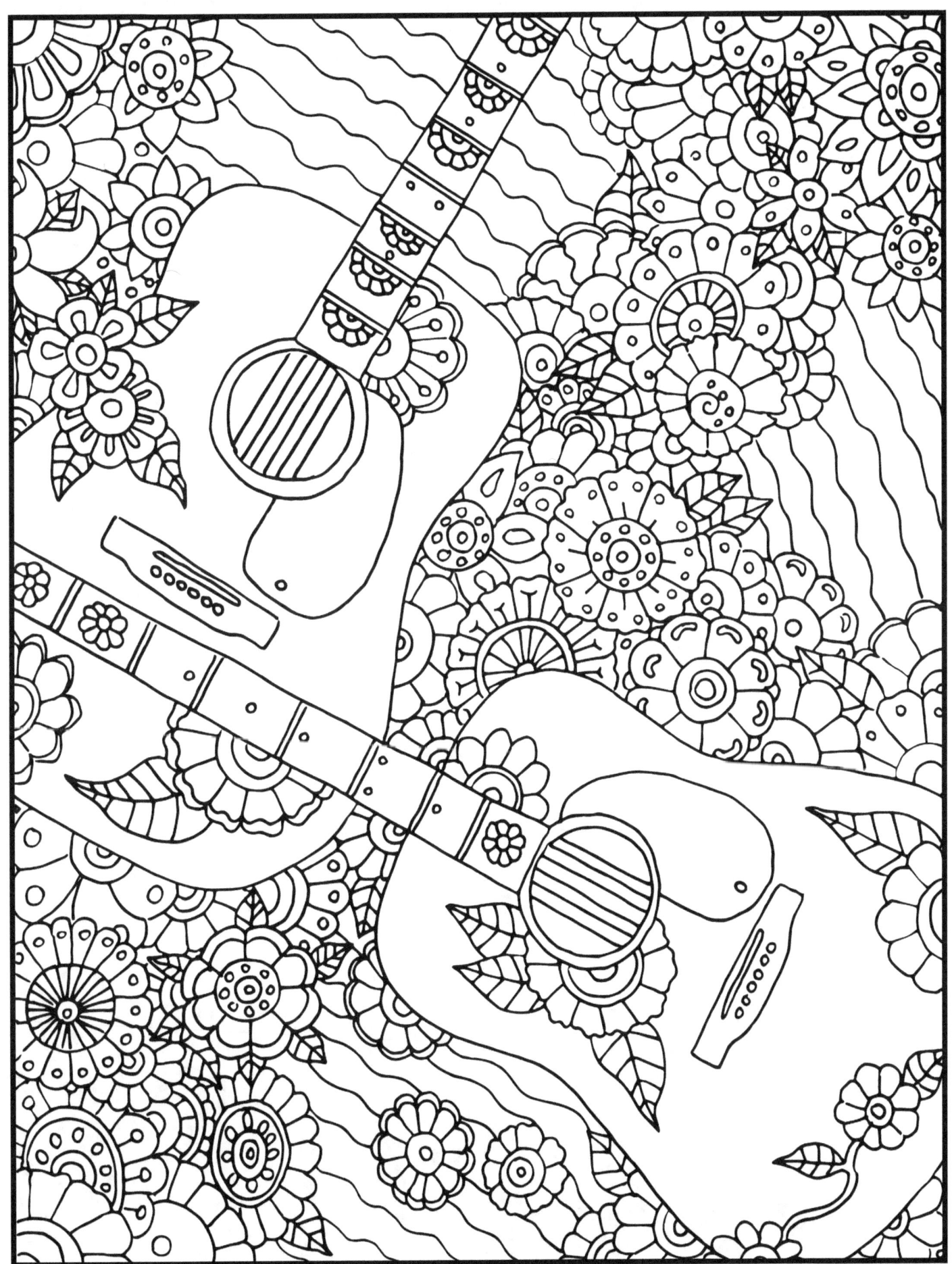

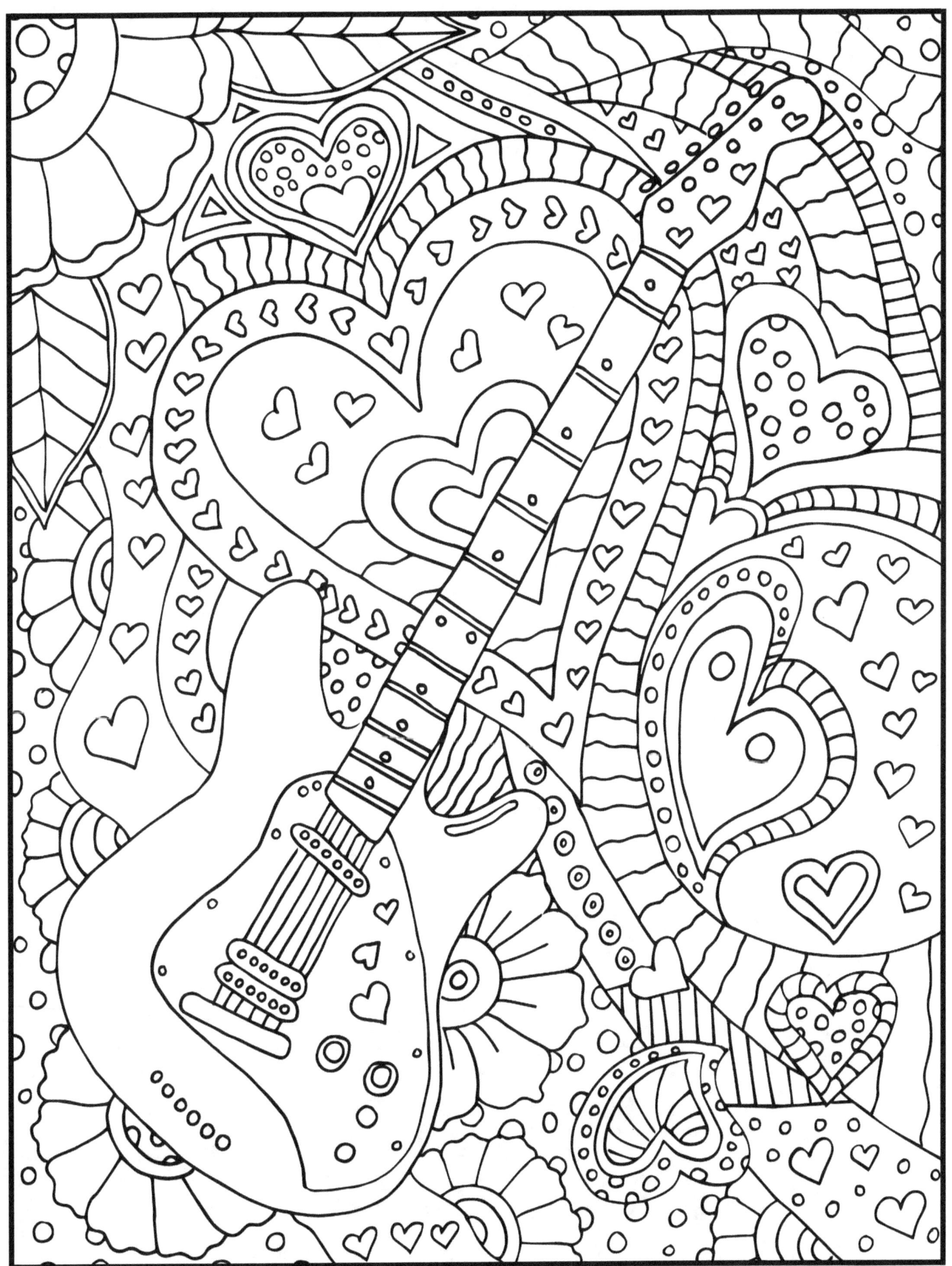

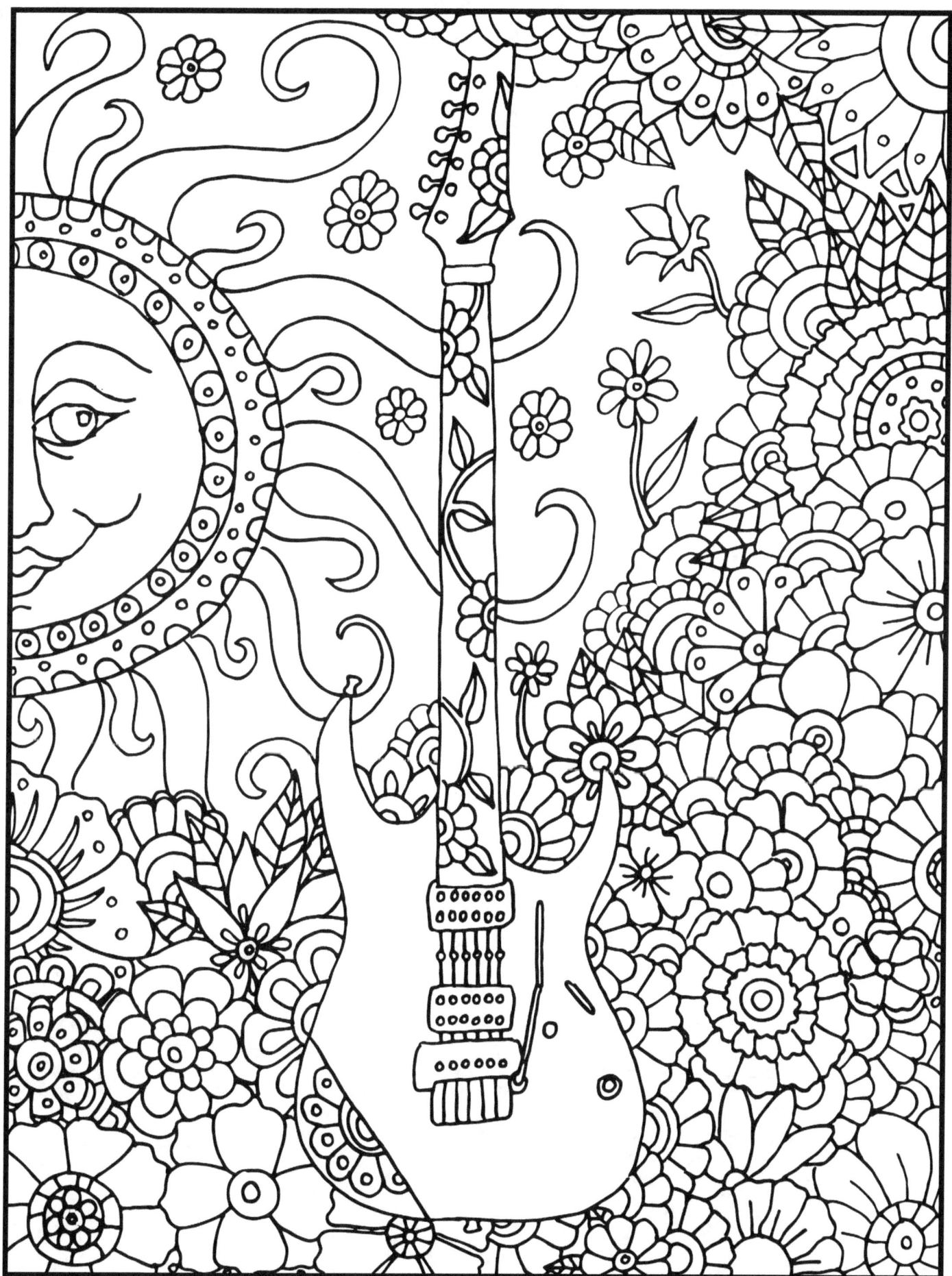

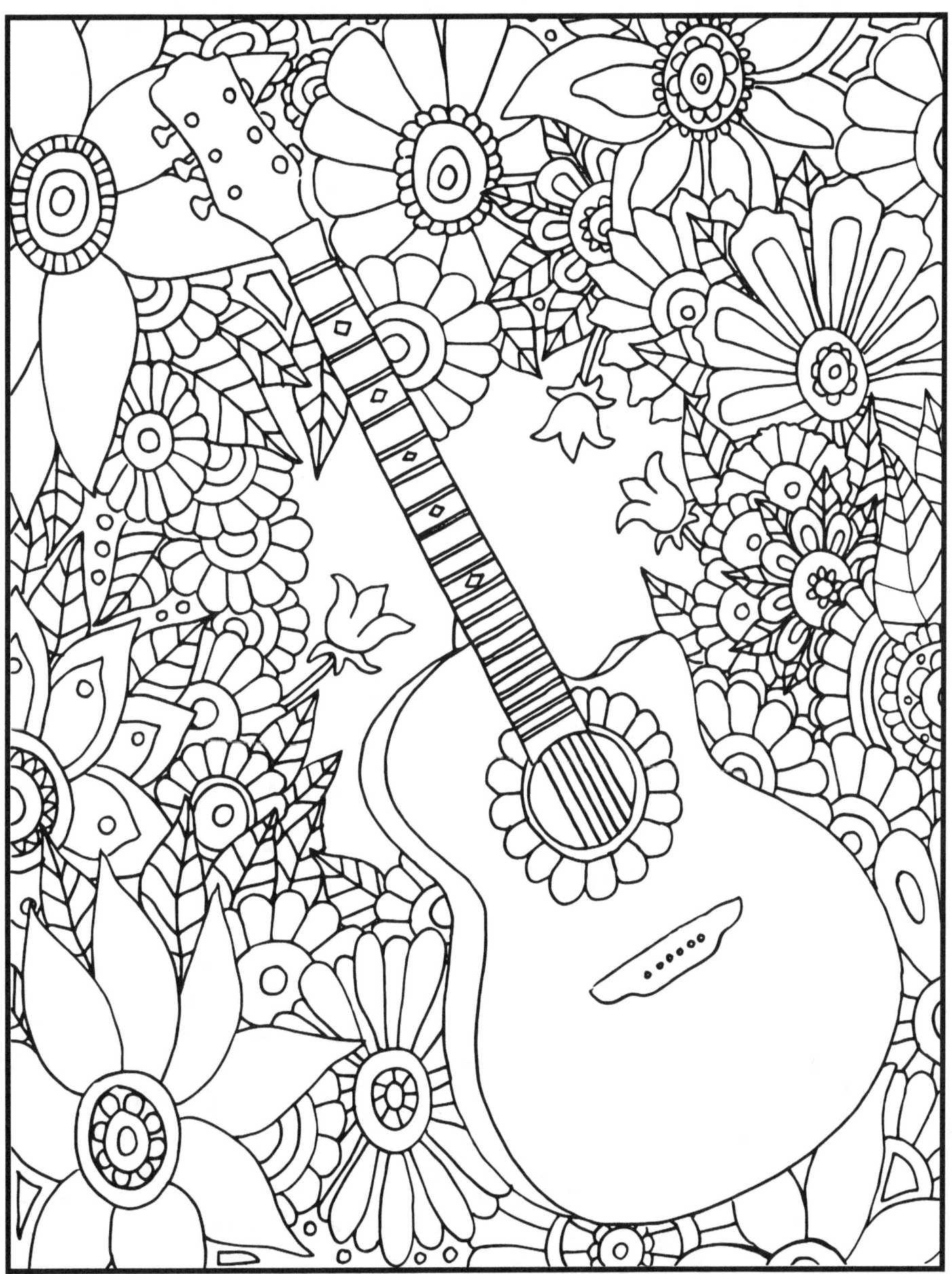

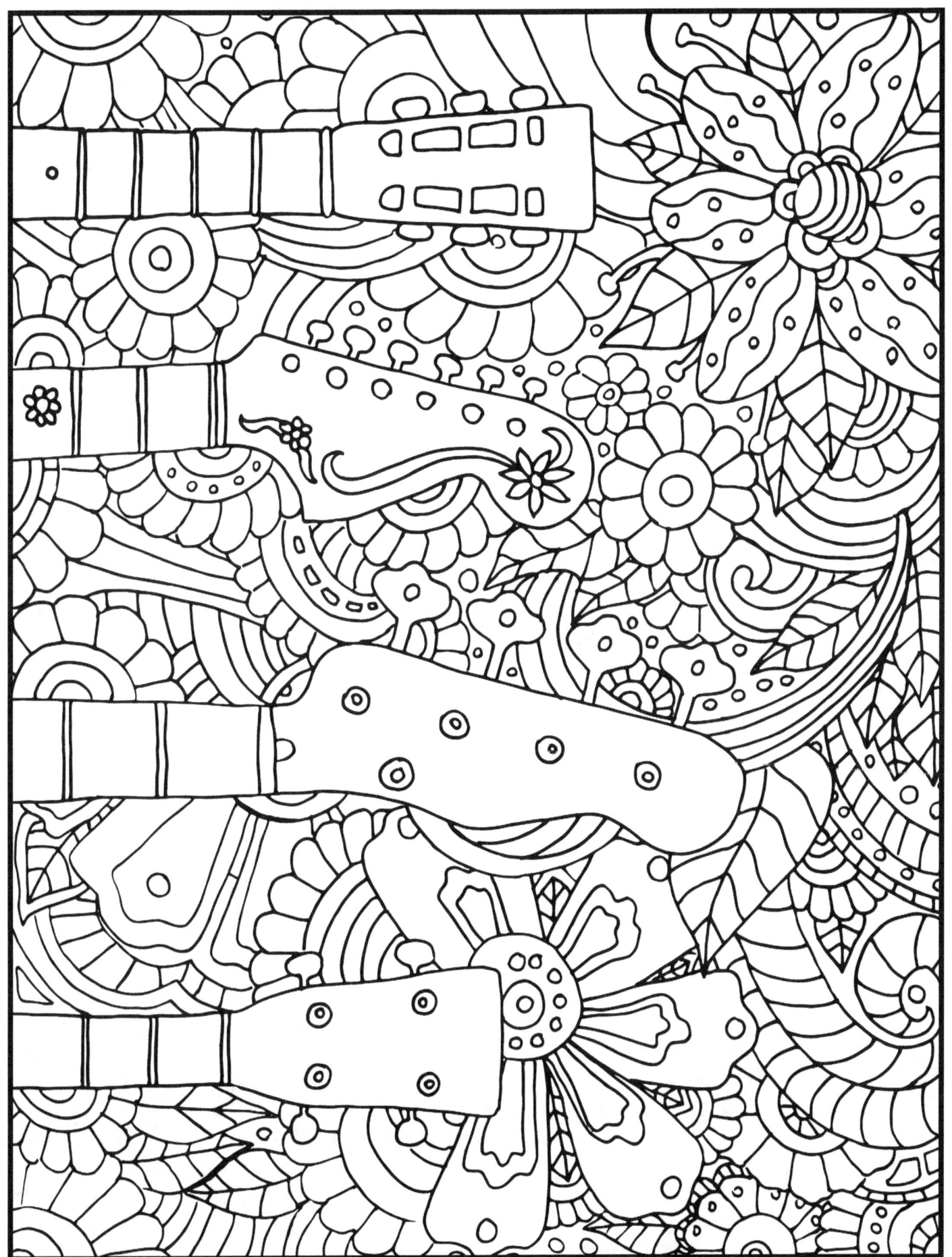

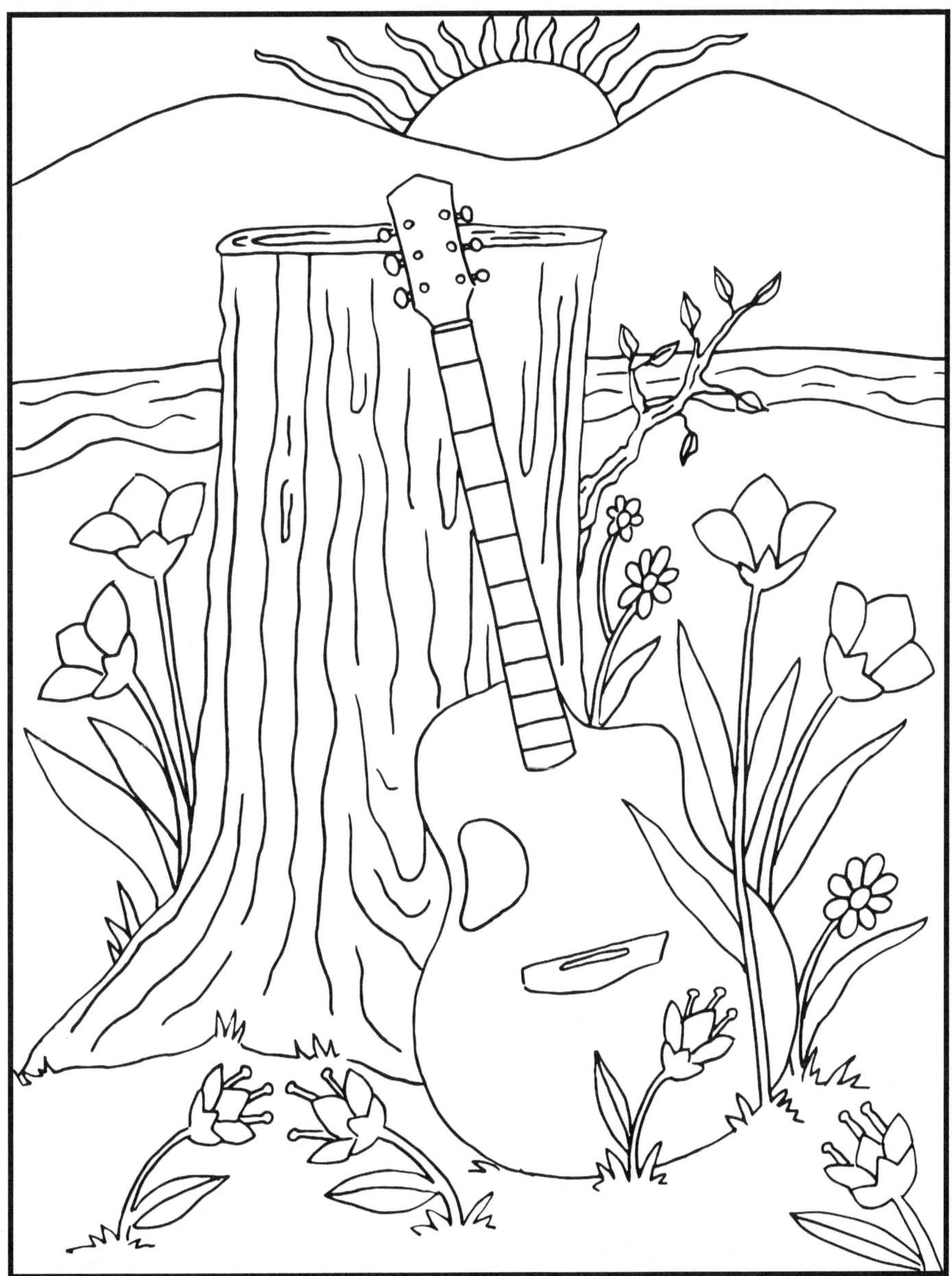

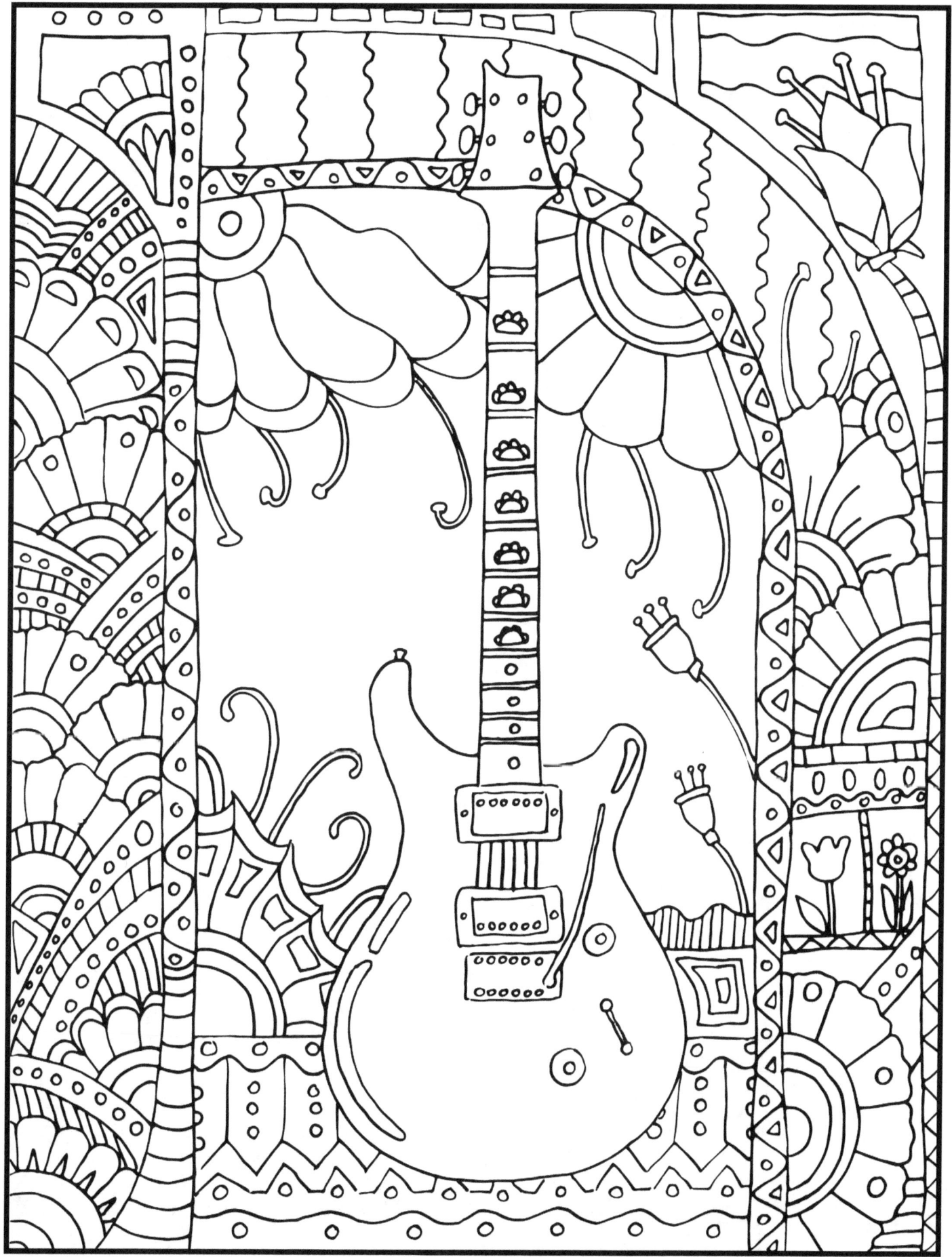

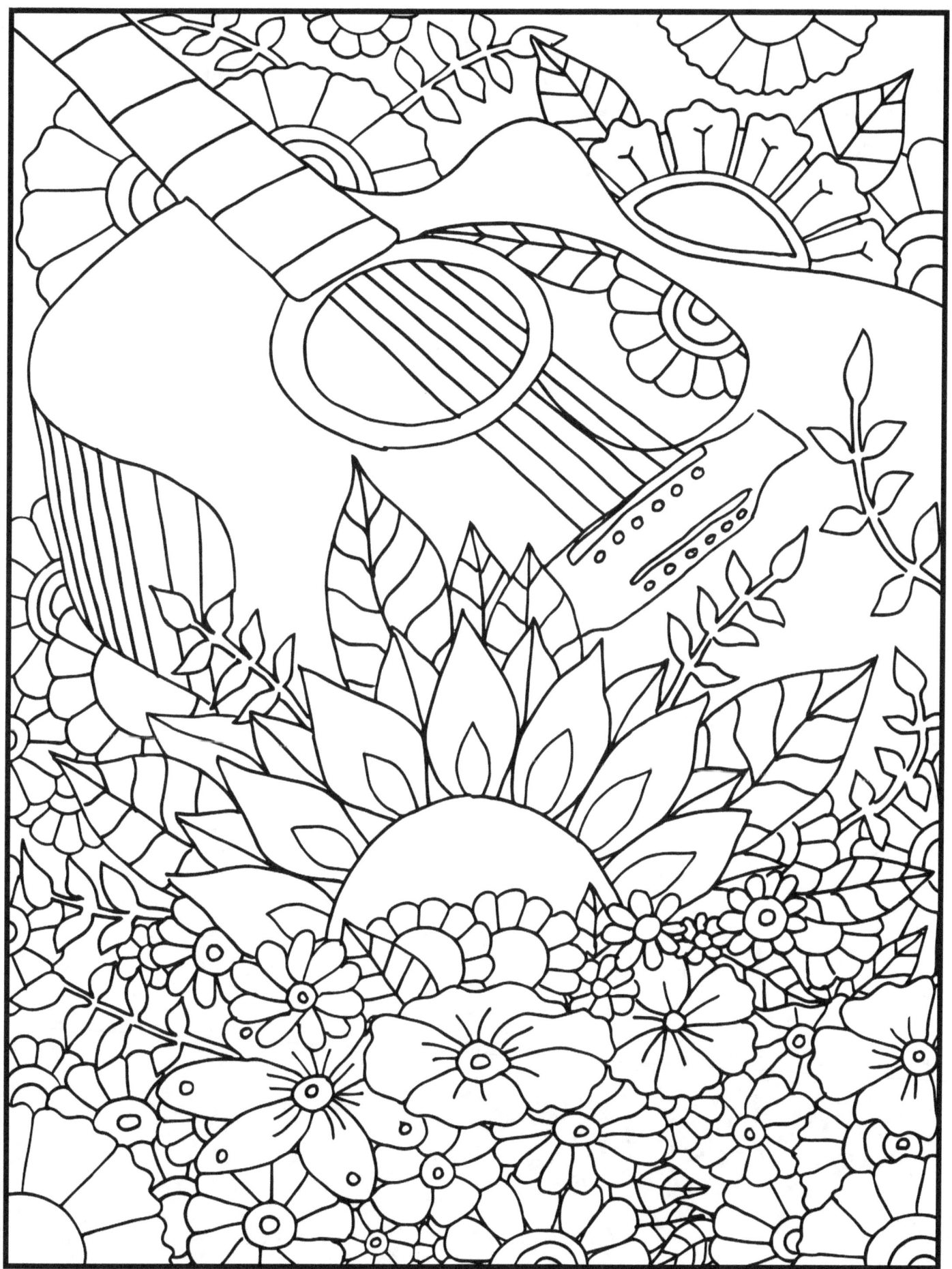

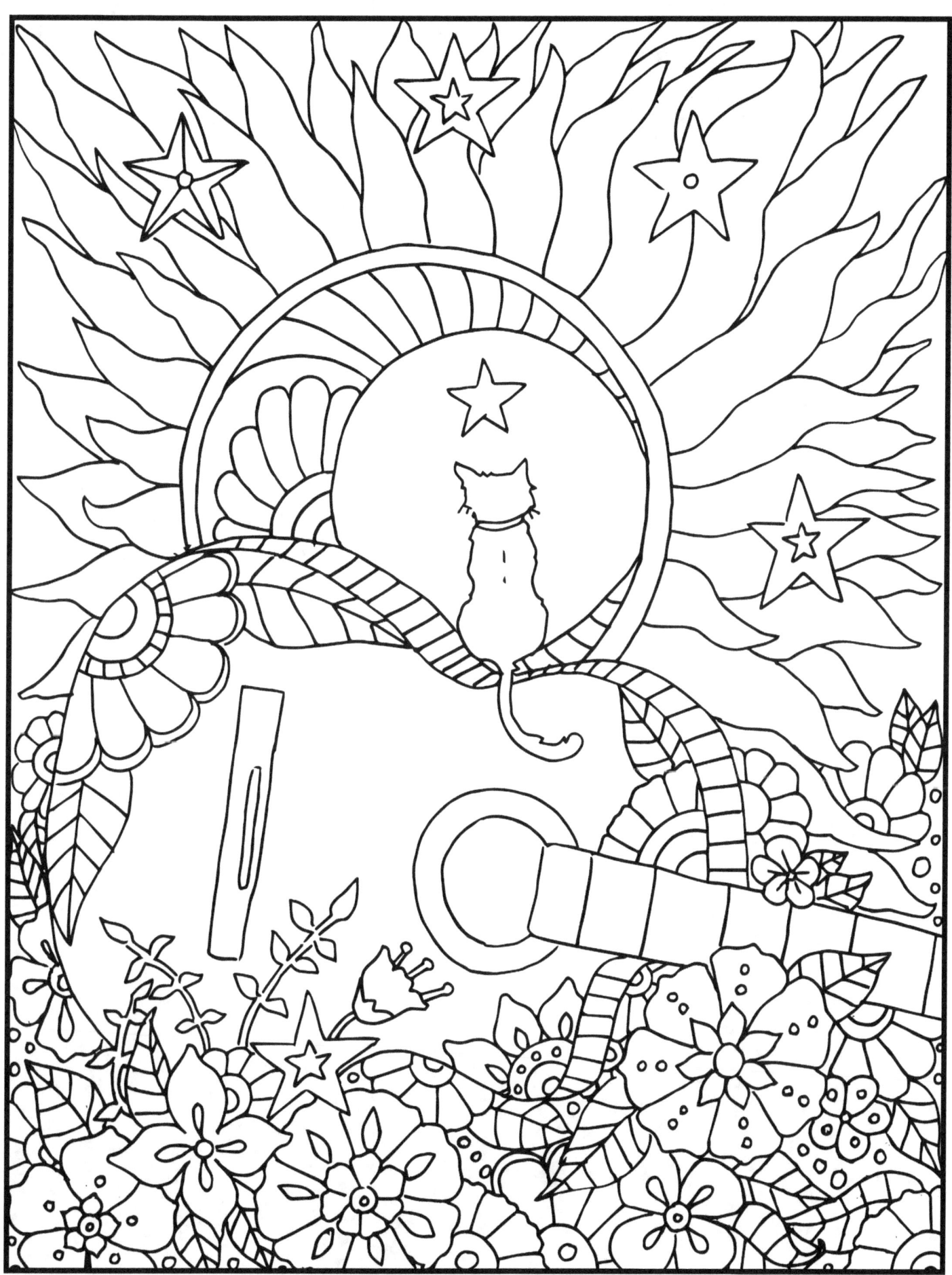

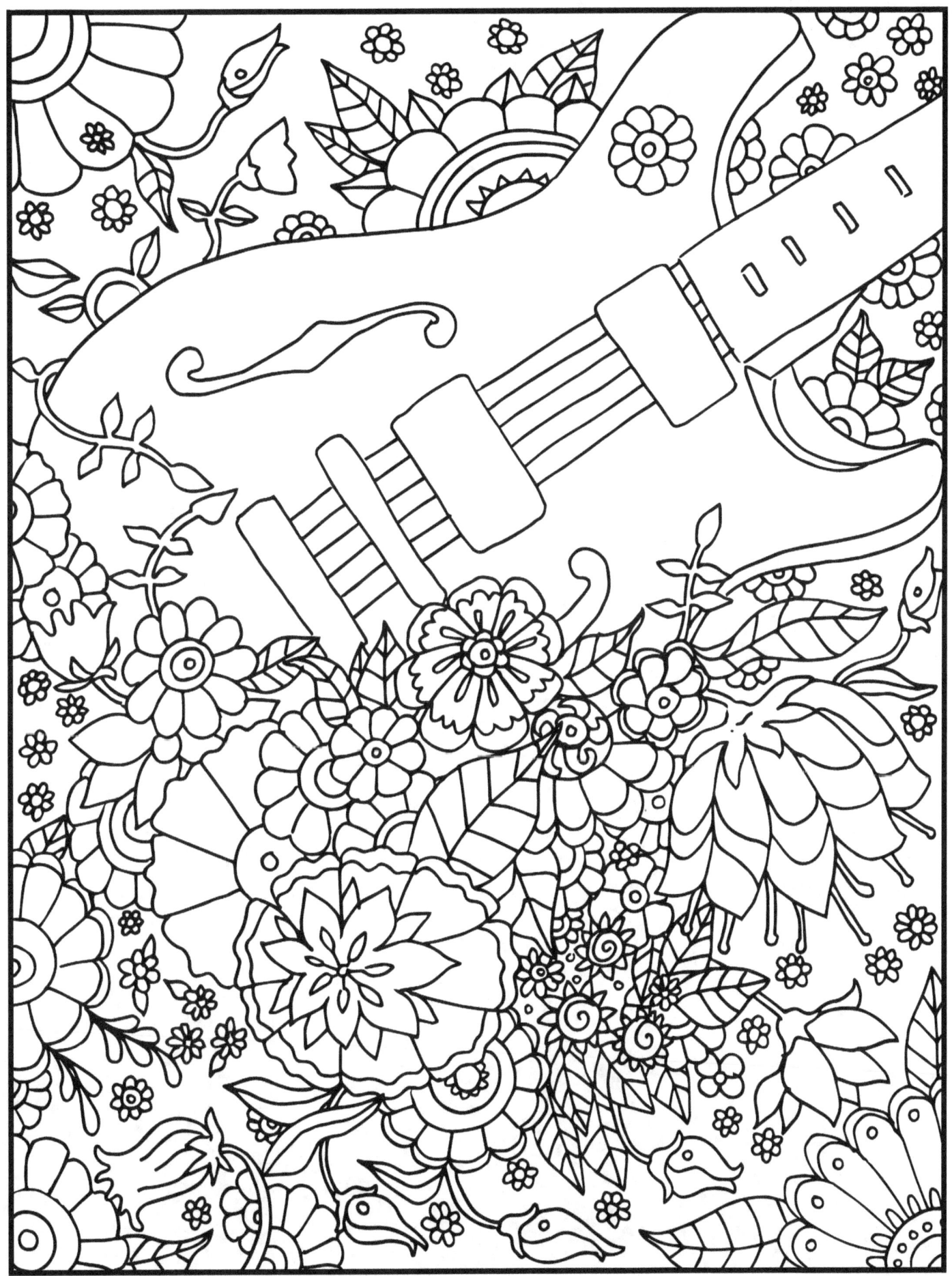

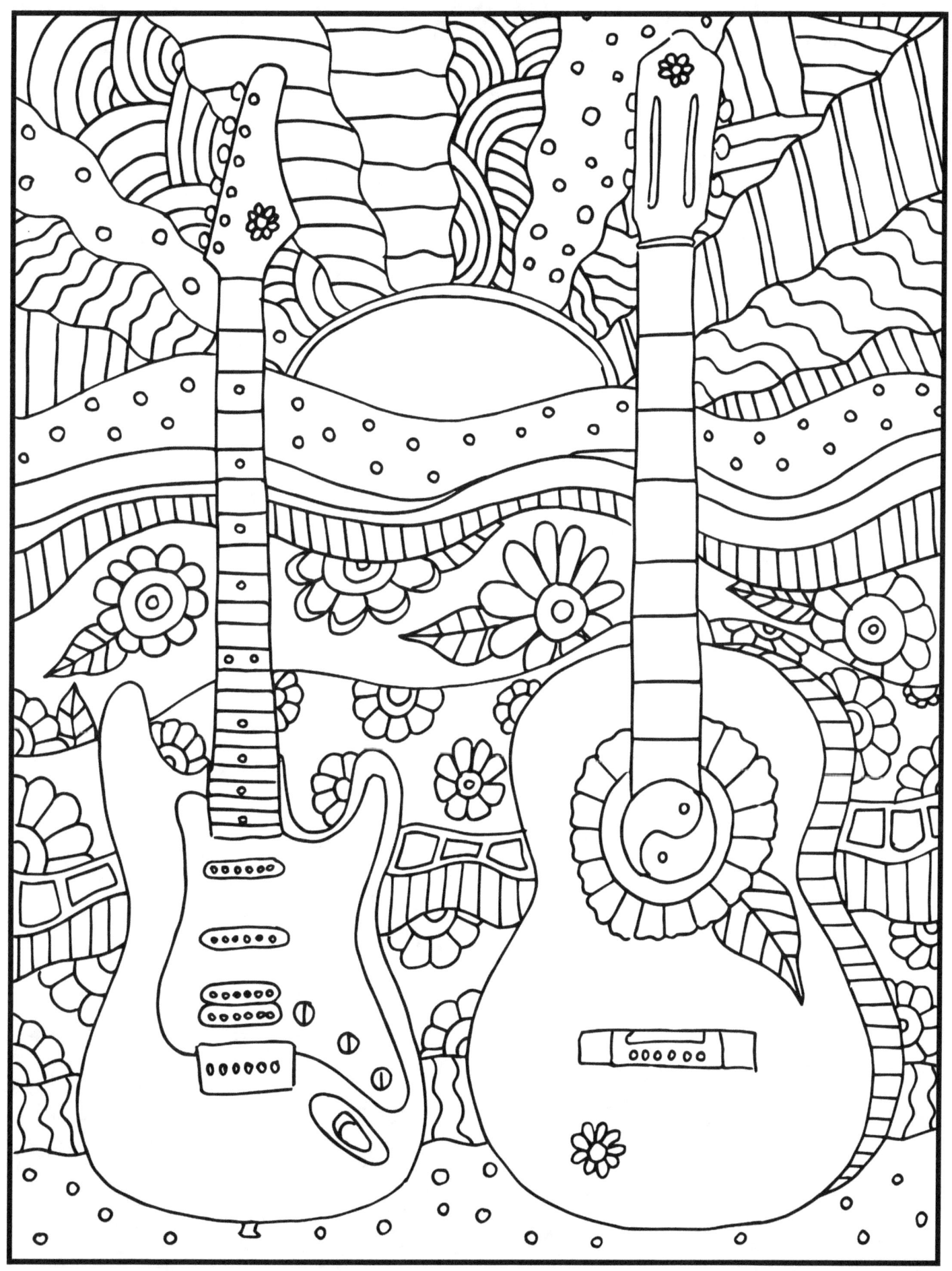

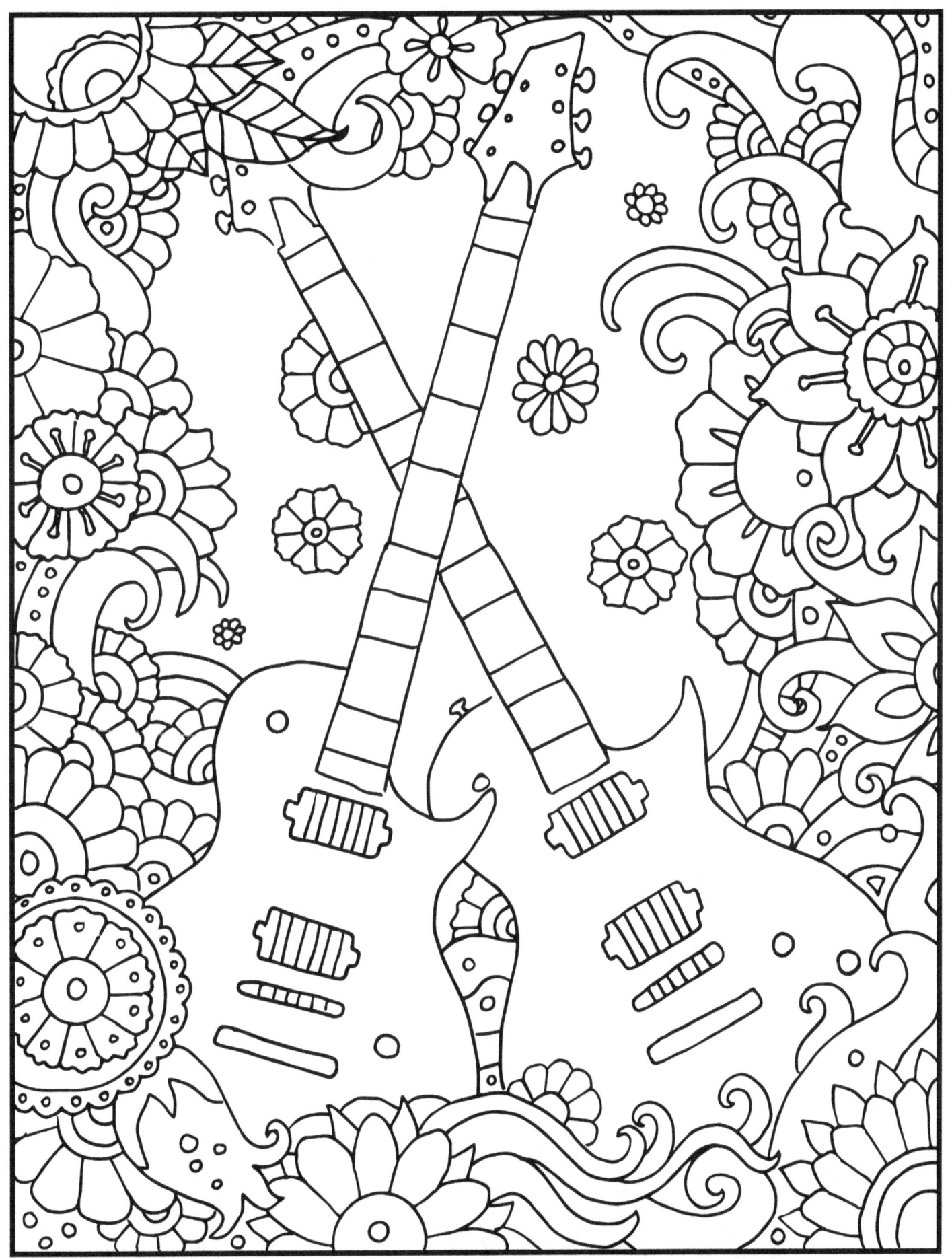

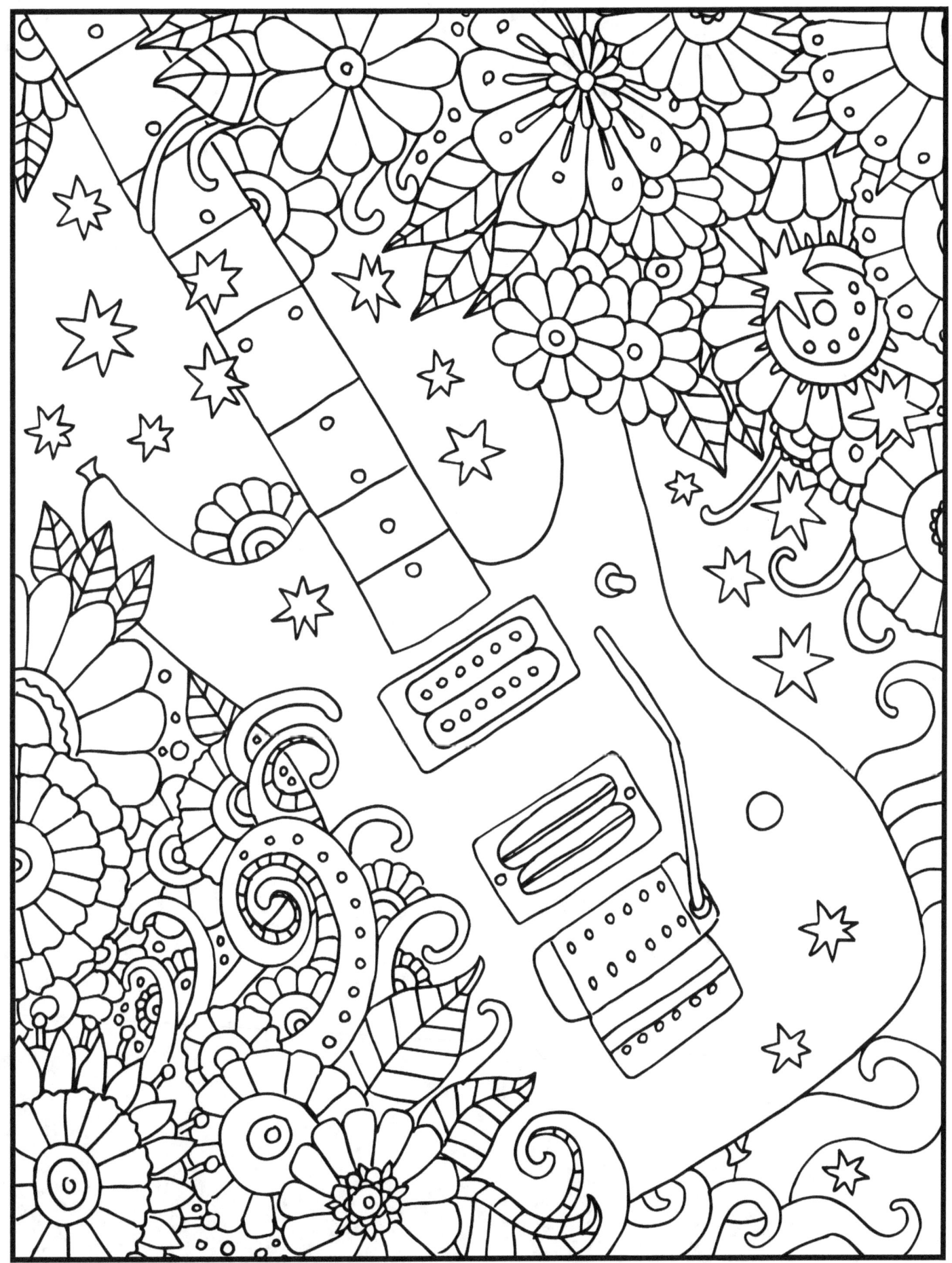

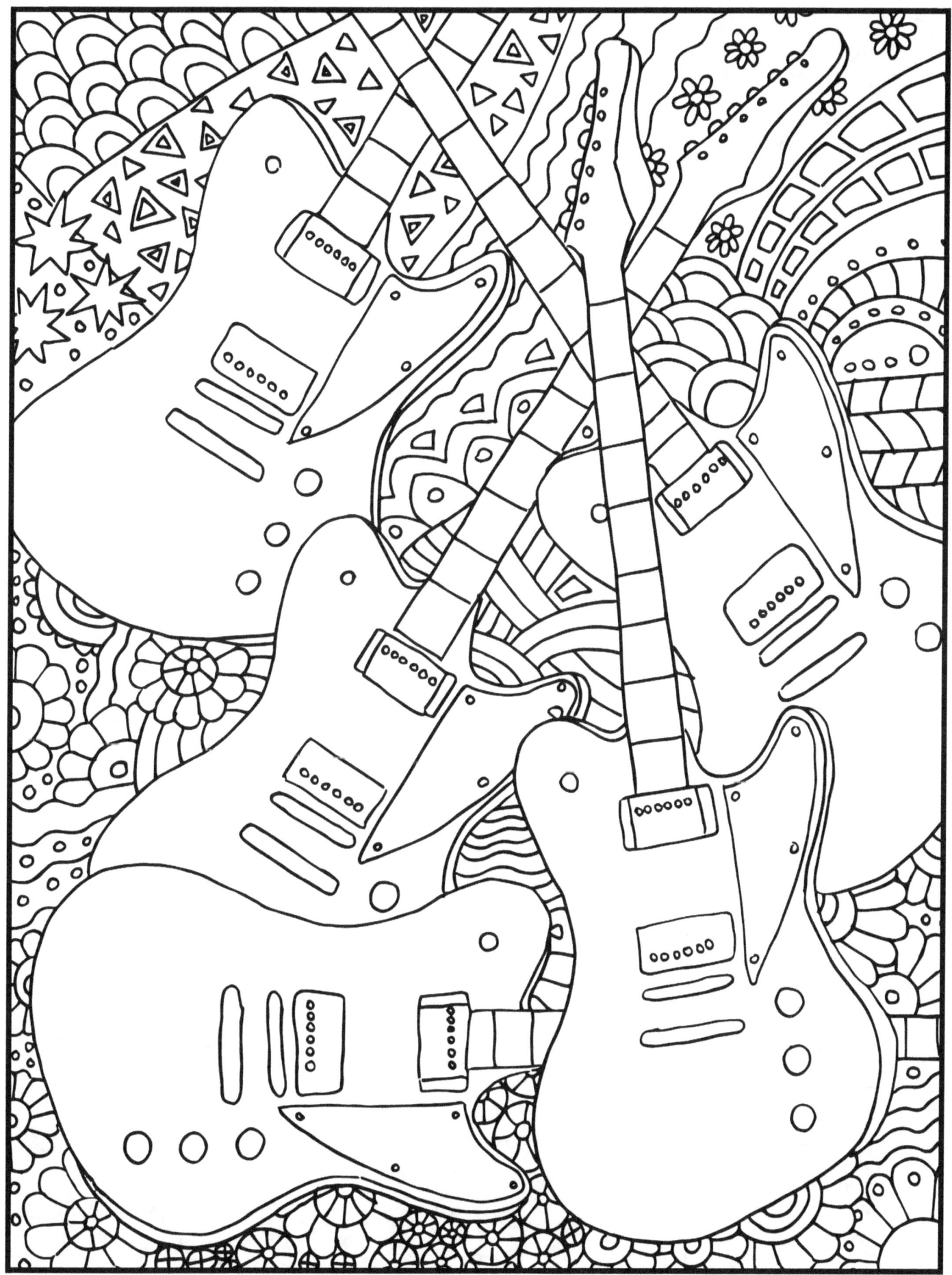

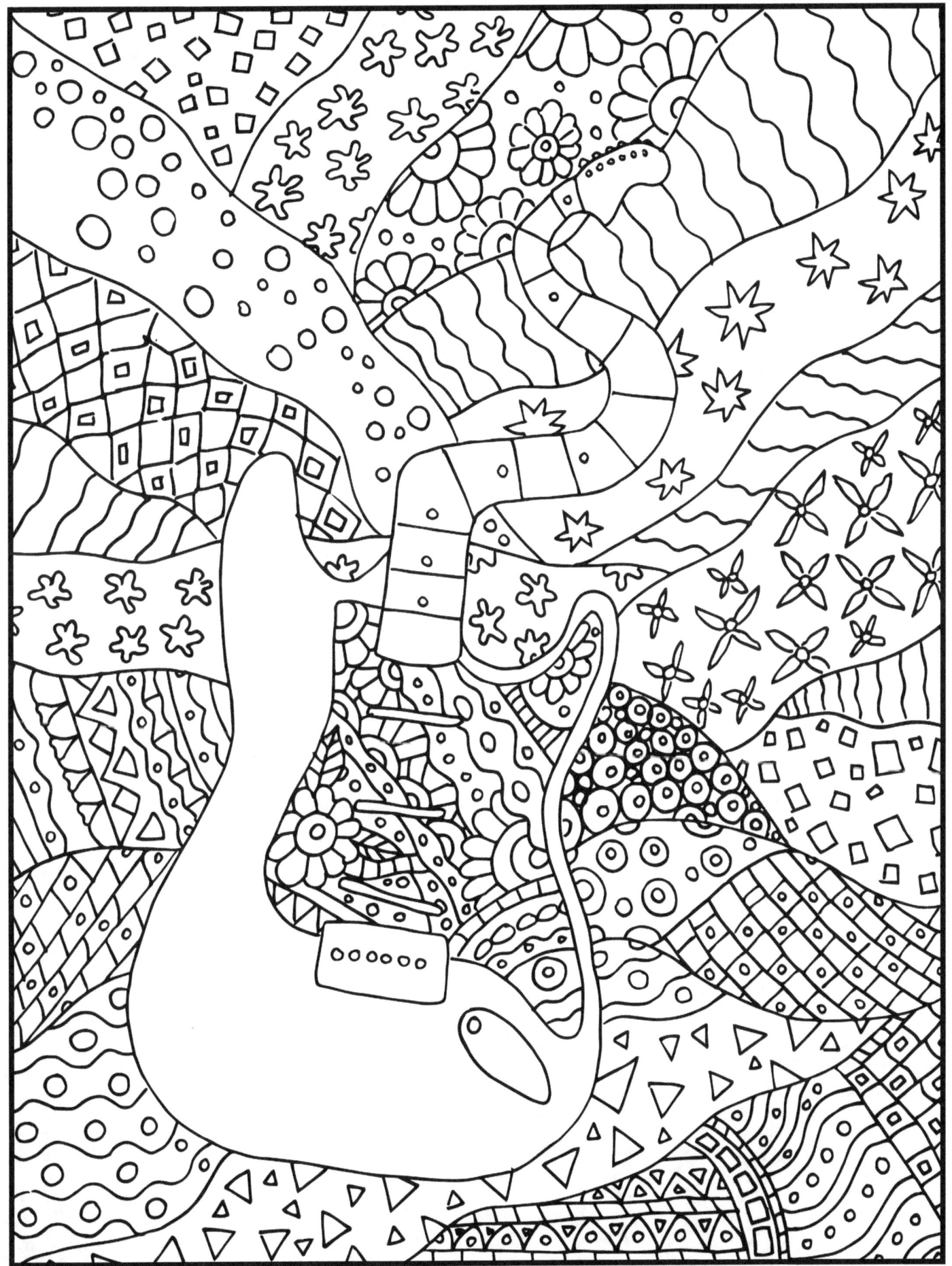

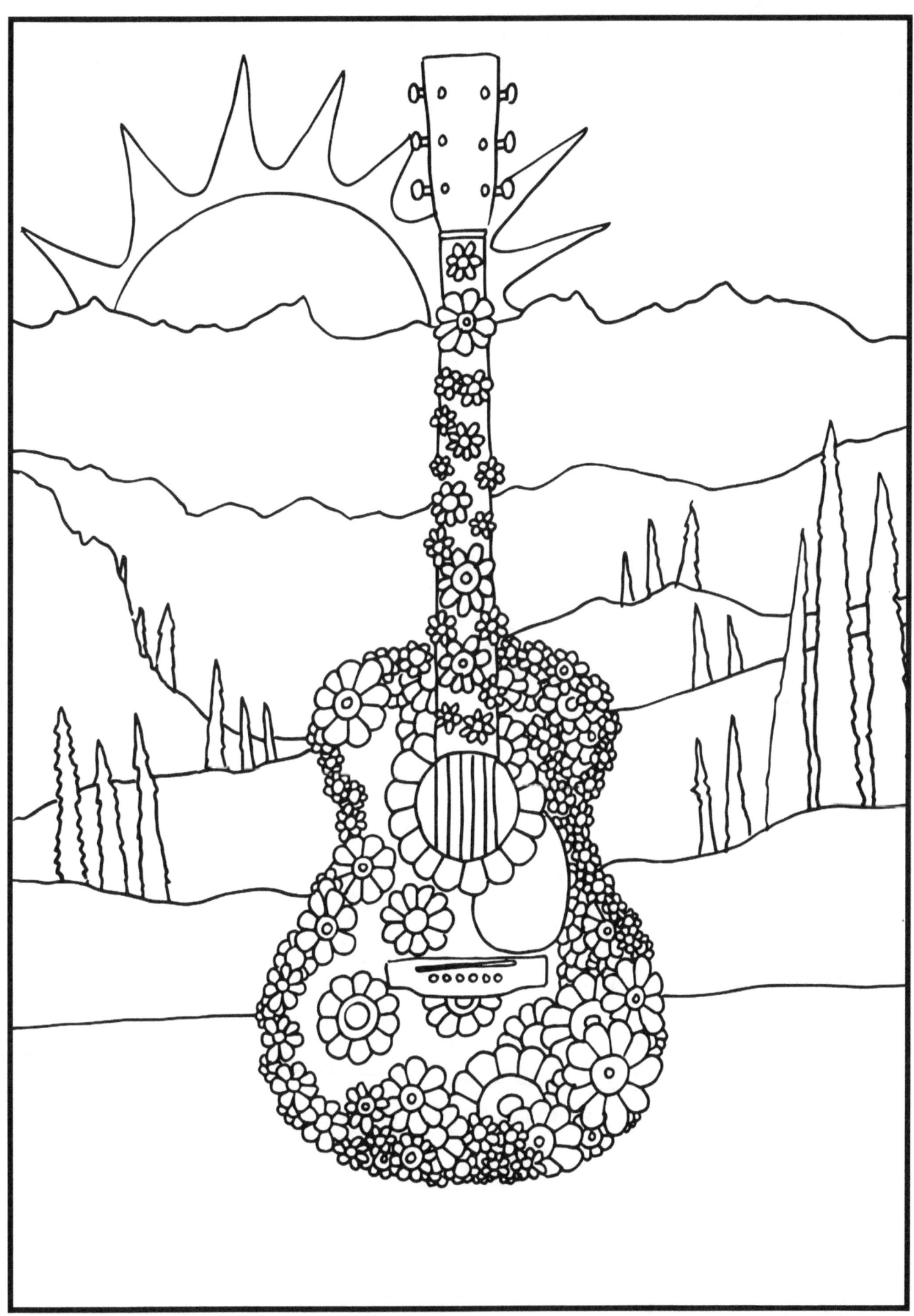

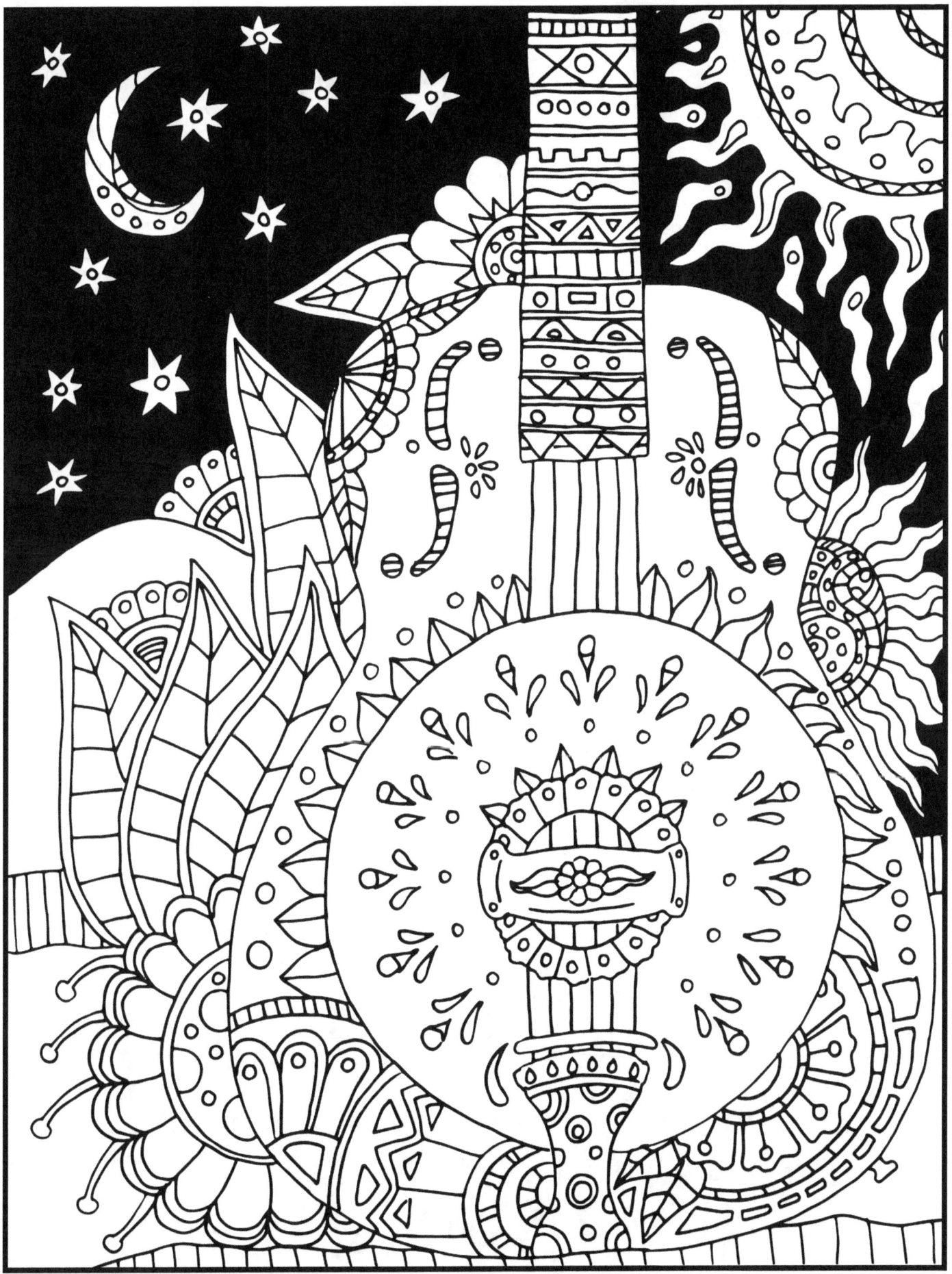

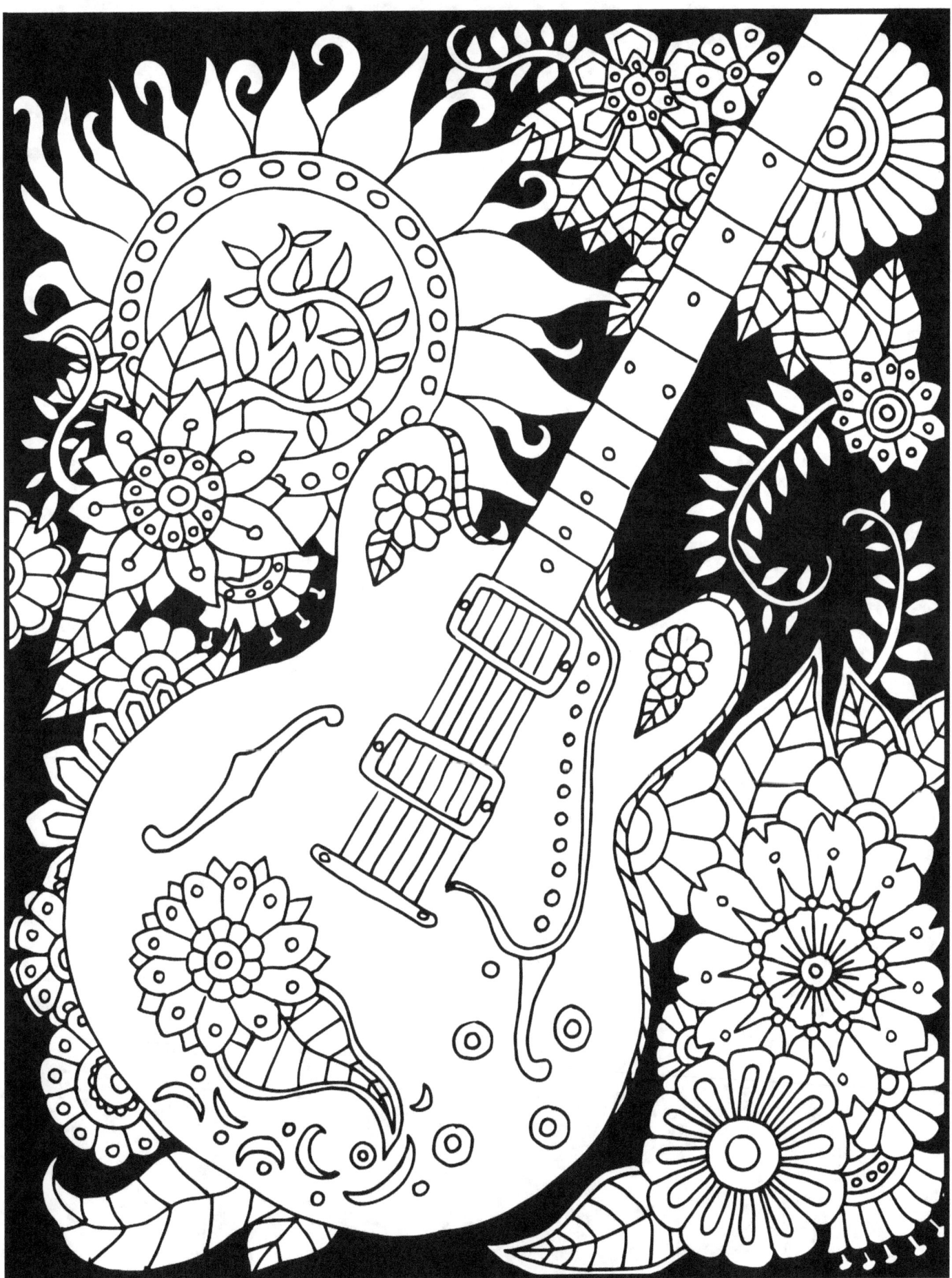

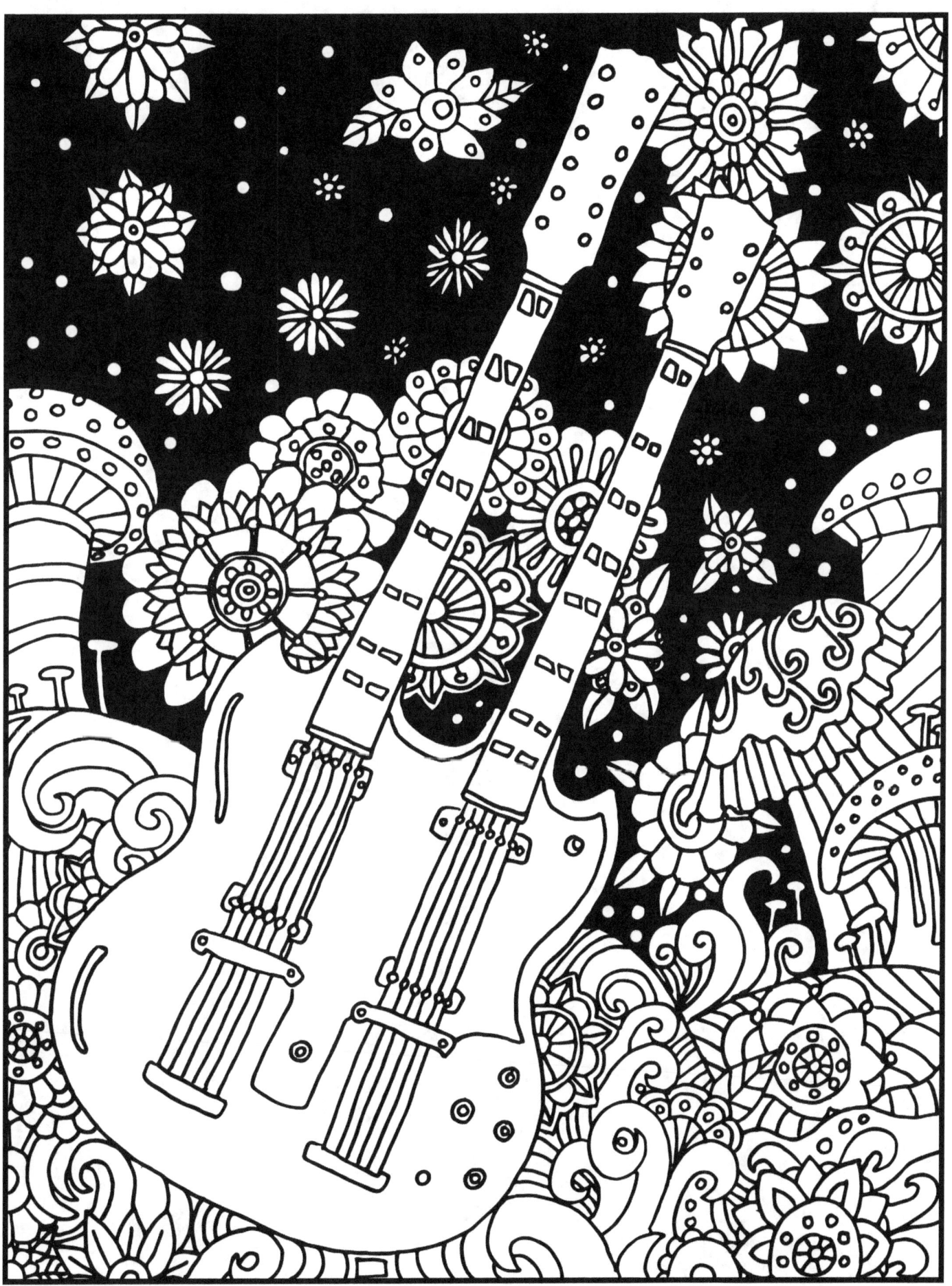

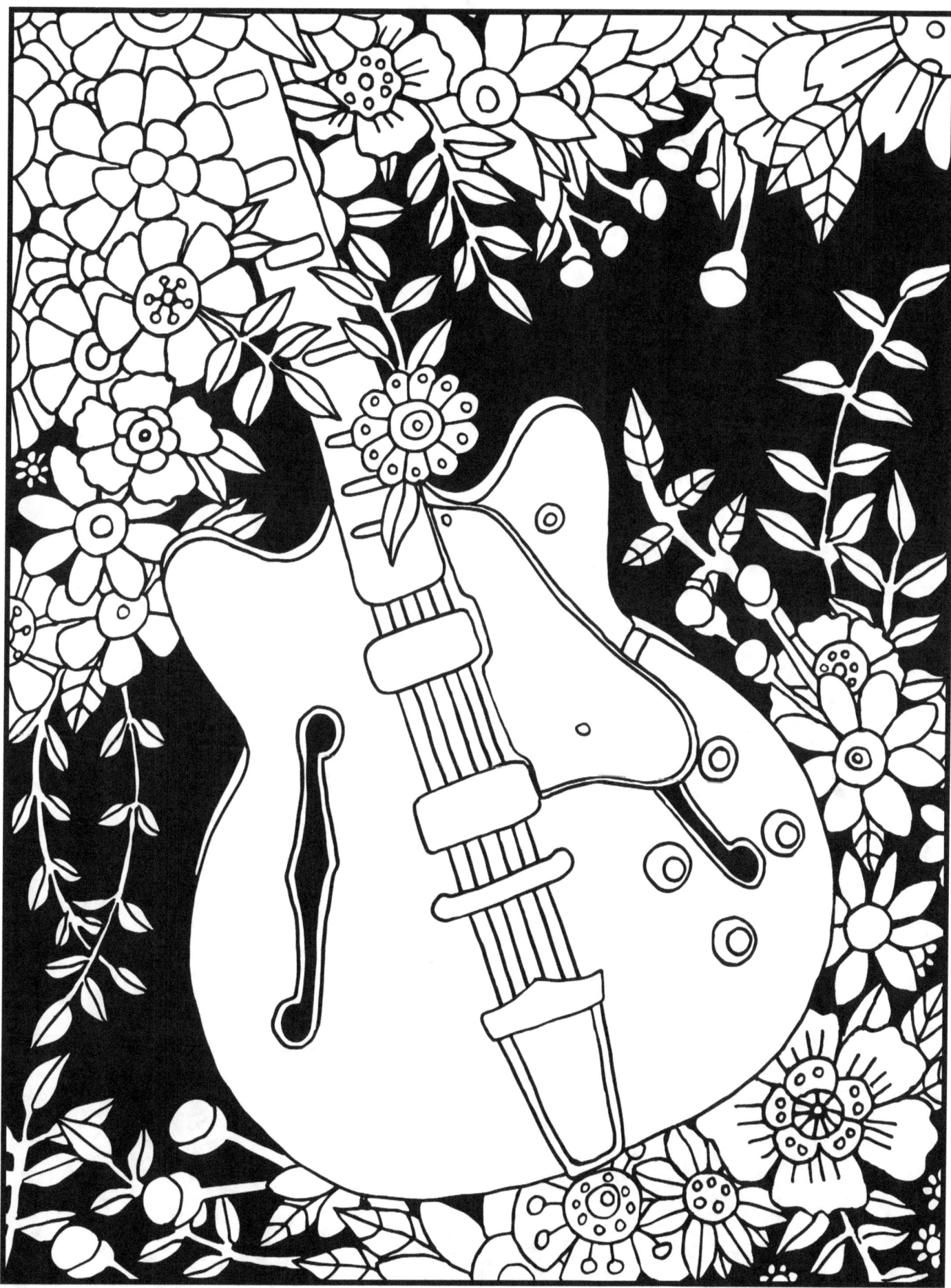

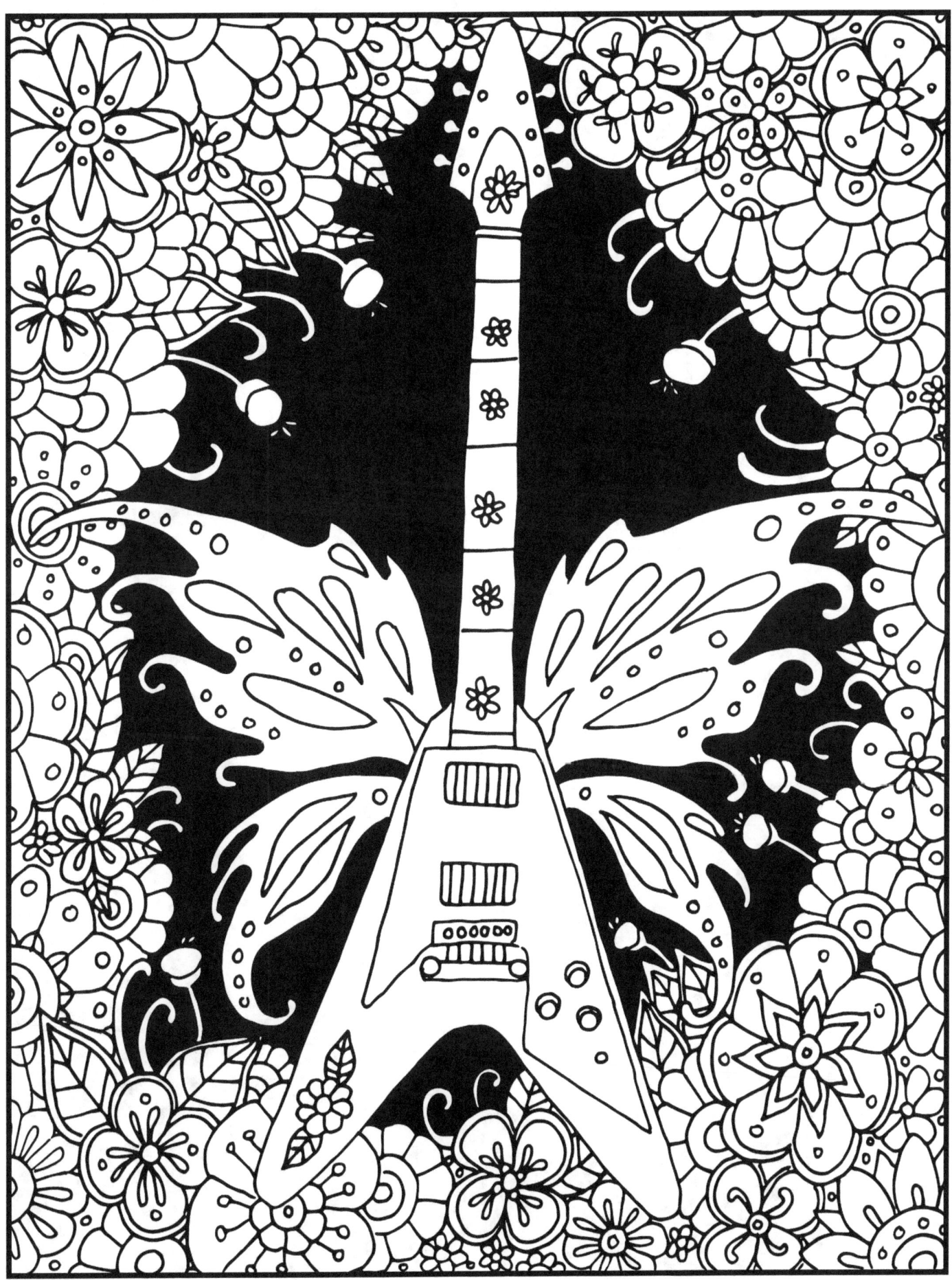

Also Available by Kimberly Garvey

- **Strange Designs** - An adult coloring book for everyone.
- **Strange Little Designs** - A mini/travel adult coloring book.
- **Simple Designs** - An adult coloring book with easier pages.
- **Simple Designs II** - An adult coloring book with easier pages.
- **Simple Little Designs** - A mini/travel sized book w/easier pages.
- **Magical Daydreams** - An adult coloring book for everyone.
- **It's Complicated** - A challenging book for the daring colorists.
- **It's Complicated II -** A more challenging coloring book.
- **It's Complicated III-** A more challenging coloring book.
- **The Fox Book** - A foxy coloring book for everyone.
- **SUPER Simple Designs -** SUPER easy adult coloring
- **SUPER Simple Designs II -** Another SUPER easy adult coloring
- **Playful Adventures** - An adult coloring book for everyone.
- **Random Designs** - Designs of various difficulty levels.
- **Alien Flowers From Another Dimension** - A coloring book for everyone.
- **I Love Hearts** - Heart themed coloring book for all.
- **Hours of Flowers** - An adult flowery coloring book.
- **Delightful Journeys**– Landscapes, places and animals.
- **Abstract Painting Coloring Book**— A different kind of grayscale
- **Color a Tree** - Tree themed coloring book
- **Inky Expressions** - An adult coloring book for everyone.
- **Kimberly's Coloring Collection** - Variety Coloring Book
- **Mushroom Magic**—Coloring Book for Everyone
- **Simple Mushroom Designs**—Easier Pages

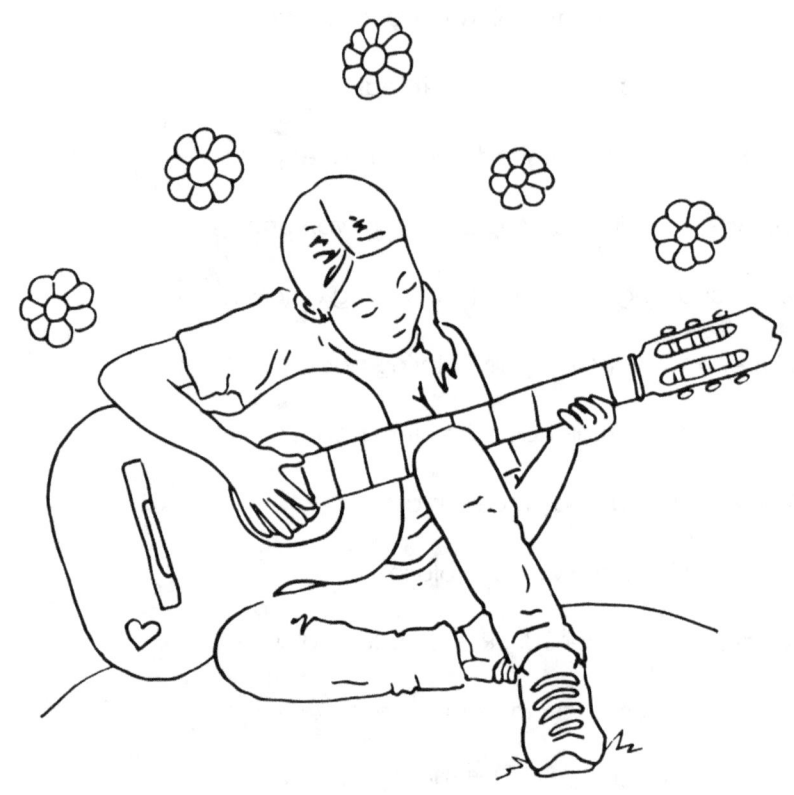

KIMBERLYGARVEY.COM

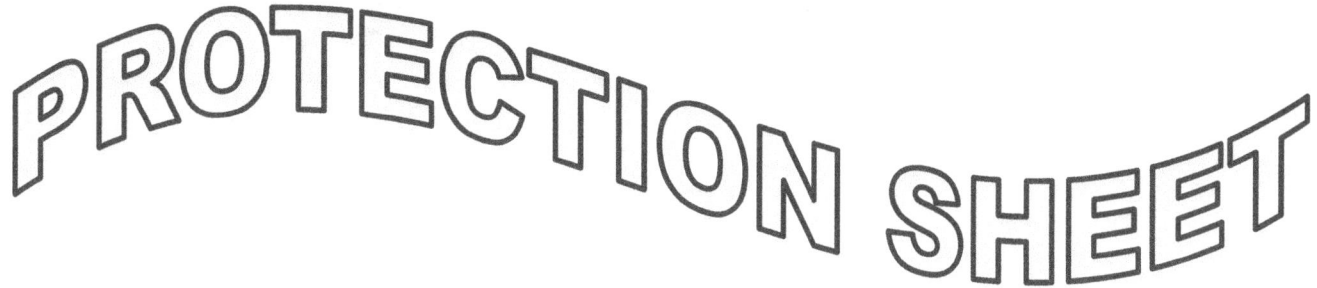

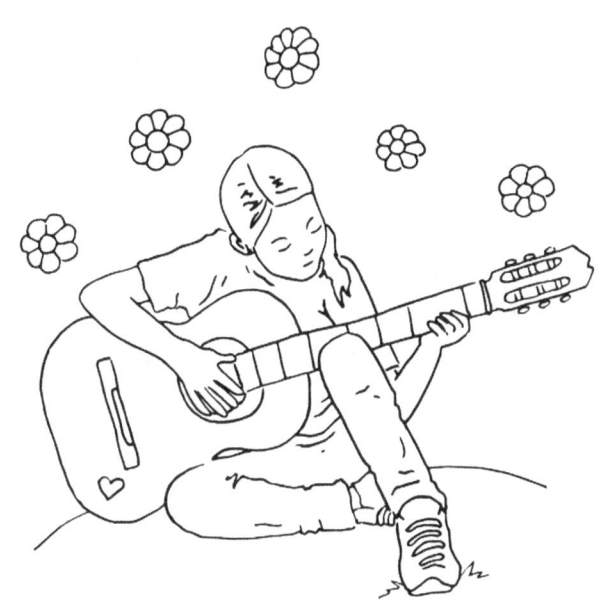

Place this page between coloring pages when using markers to prevent bleed-through.

KIMBERLYGARVEY.COM

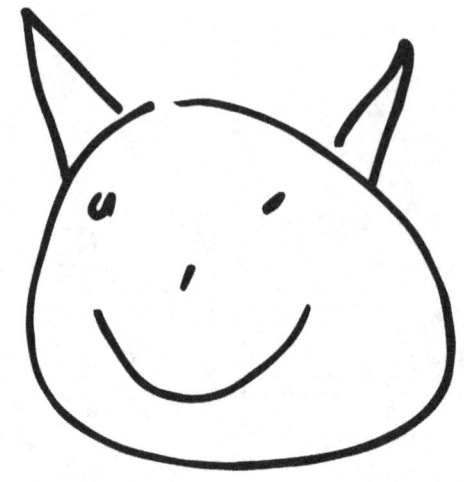

KIMBERLYGARVEY.COM